# MOUNTAIN BIKE RIDES

## IN THE COLORADO FRONT RANGE

# MOUNTAIN BIKE RIDES
## IN THE COLORADO FRONT RANGE

WILLIAM L. STOEHR

PRUETT

PRUETT PUBLISHING COMPANY
BOULDER, COLORADO

Copyright 1988 by William L. Stoehr

**Library of Congress Cataloging-in-Publication Data**

Stoehr, William L., 1948 -
    Mountain bike rides in the Colorado Front Range

    1. Bicycle touring — Front Range (Colo. and Wyo.) — Guide-books.   2. Front Range (Colo. and Wyo.) — Description and travel — Guide-books.   I. Title.
GV1045.5.F76S75      1988          917.88'3          88-9861
ISBN 0-87108-740-5 (pbk.)

First Edition
  2 3 4 5 6 7 8 9

Printed in the United States of America.

*All photographs courtesy of the author.*

*Design & Typography —*
    Richard M. Kohen      Shadow Canyon Graphics - Evergreen, Colorado

# Contents

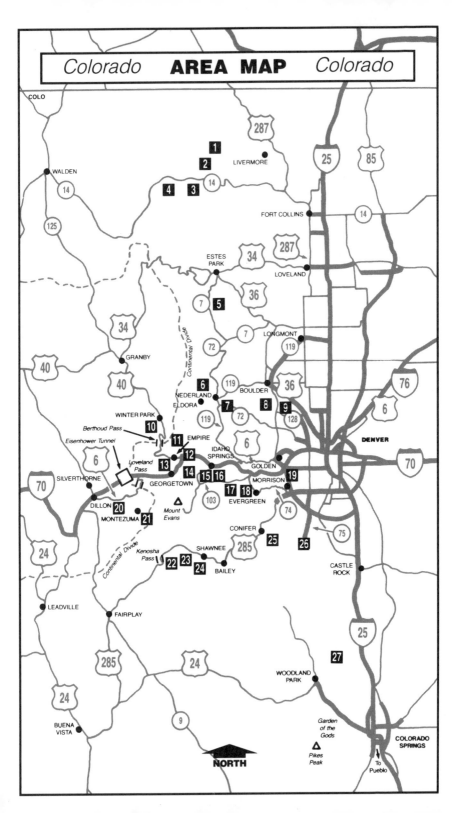

NORTH

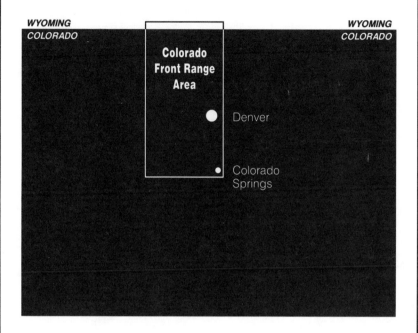

WYOMING
COLORADO

WYOMING
COLORADO

Colorado
Front Range
Area

Denver

Colorado
Springs

*To my best friends —*
*Mary and Greg.*

*We came to the mountains*
*for adventure.*

*We stayed and found*
*understanding, harmony,*
*and love.*

# Introduction

So here you are with Friday afternoon off and a bug to hit the trail. Where can you ride without missing supper? Well, many of the Front Range area rides in this book are easy to get to and just as easy to finish before rush hour.

The mountain biking boom is on. The sport is here to stay. In Colorado over half of all bikes sold are mountain bikes. The construction of the bike — the heavy-duty frame, the fat tires, the cantilever brakes, the additional gears — allows you to go where a ten speed cannot. The upright riding position is comfortable and great for mountain watching. Think of a mountain bike as an amalgamation of a light-weight ten-speed racer and a balloon-tire paperboy bike.

Mountain bikers ride on pavement, mining roads, jeep trails, hiking trails, and dirt. Their increasing presence on the last two is causing dissention. The controversy is over the use of mountain bikes on public land. While about half of the land in Colorado is government owned, almost all of the prime recreational land is government owned.

Specifically, the key issues are: the potential for environmental damage, the aesthetic impact of mountain bikes on wilderness areas and other trails where hikers and wildlife are present, and equal access to recreational areas for mountain bikers.

In general, Colorado state, county, and local government roads and trails may be legally used by mountain bikers. The same is true of federally owned land, with the exception of wilderness areas and some National Park trails. In 1964 Congress passed the Wilderness Act, which was intended to preserve certain pristine areas. Section 4(c) of the Wilderness Act prohibits the use of all forms of "mechanical transport" in wilderness areas. The National Forest Service is responsible for the enforcement of the Wilderness Act in twenty-five of Colorado's twenty-eight wilderness areas, and they have interpreted "mechanical transport" to include bicycles. There is also a strong sentiment for further restrictions in areas not covered by the Wilderness Act.

Some people are concerned that mountain bikes will damage our fragile wilderness areas and trails. I suspect that a responsible mountain biker does less damage to a trail than a horse does, but shouldn't the issue be one of preventing additional damage of any kind? Maybe we should be working to ban horses from wilderness areas. Large equestrian parties do an incredible amount of trail damage, and after all, a string of dudes is hardly a natural occurrence in the wilderness.

If we are to preserve wilderness areas we must minimize our impact on them — period. Mountain biking is a fast-growing new sport. More riders have the potential to do more damage. People see what the motorized crowd did to the Rampart Range and now they are running scared — I don't blame them. Comparing a mountain bike to a motorized all-terrain vehicle is unfair and probably just political posturing — but face it, there is the potential for more damage as the sport grows.

Aesthetic impact is another controversial and misunderstood issue. What this means is that if I am hiking in the woods, I do not want you to zip by me on a bike. This mechanical intrusion is incongruous with my wilderness experience. For many, preservation of the wilderness experience is the primary reason for the Wilderness Act. Remember, good backpacking is more dependent on the wilderness than is good mountain biking. A lone biker on a deserted trail does not intrude. But where do you draw the line?

Equal access is a nonissue. The real issue should be equal opportunity. Let me say this another way. I pay taxes that help support the local high school girl's volleyball team. I can't join the team. Just because you pay taxes don't expect equal access to the wilderness and other environmentally sensitive areas, or to popular hiking trails. What mountain bikers can expect and should fight for is an equal opportunity to responsibly pursue their sport. There are alternative places to ride. It's time to develop some of these for mountain bikers.

There is a hiker/biker conflict. There is an environmental concern. But here in Colorado, provide for equal opportunity outside of environmentally sensitive and heavily used areas, and you can solve the problem.

One approach is to legislate and administer a solution. Another approach is to make mountain bikers aware of the problem, and then provide information regarding attractive alternative mountain bike routes. Hence this book.

The Colorado Front Range is replete with backcountry roads, ways, old mining roads, and jeep trails that are available to mountain bikers and easy to get to. Taking advantage of that, I have outlined some environmentally acceptable Front Range routes too tough for a ten speed, yet negotiable with a mountain bike. There is a continuum of routes — easy and beginning to strenuous and technically challenging. I have included historical and geological tidbits, plus information regarding trees, flowers, plants, fishing holes, supplementary route spurs, and available facilities.

# How to Buy a Mountain Bike

Not all fat-tire bikes are mountain bikes. A true mountain bike may cost as little as $250 or as much as $3000. Many good mountain bikes fall into the $300 to $700 range. Unless you have a special requirement, or unless you have a burning desire to stimulate the economy, $300 to $700 will get you through any backcountry tour.

The difference between a $300 and a $700 mountain bike may be as tangible as sealed bearings and frame geometry, or as intangible as color and name. But to qualify as a true mountain bike it must have a heavy-duty frame, light alloy, not steel, wheels, fifteen or more speeds, cantilever or roller cam brakes, and at least 26 × 1.75 fat tires.

Mountain bikes in the $300 to $700 price range typically have a chrome-molybdenum alloy steel frame. This frame is light, yet it has the strength to take the bumps with the flexibility to ease the ride.

Light alloy wheels are lighter than steel, and they provide a better braking surface in wet weather. Believe it or not, it is easier to push an extra ounce of frame than it is to push an extra ounce of wheel. When it comes to performance, lightweight wheels are more important than a lightweight frame.

Cantilever brakes pull up from both sides of the brake assembly rather than just from the top of the brake. Mechanically speaking, cantilever brakes have a longer lever arm and can apply more force to the pads. Some bikes in the upper end of our price range may come with a rear roller cam brake and a front cantilever brake, or with both front and rear roller cam brakes. Roller cam brakes have a cam plate that pulls up between a set of rollers, forcing the pads against the rim. Here again mechanical advantage is employed to increase braking power. High performance brakes are a safety must if you plan to ride in the hills.

Mountain bikes have a three-gear chainring set versus two for a conventional ten-speed bike. This gives you at least fifteen speeds, with some very low gears to get you up steep grades and over rocks. Some come with a six-sprocket rear freewheel cluster for eighteen speeds. Five sprockets give you fifteen speeds. Finally, those fat tires cushion the ride, protect the wheels, and give you increased traction. Fat tire flat tires are relatively rare.

Mountain bike frames are constructed, measured, and sized differently than conventional ten-speed bikes. For starters, you must be able to get both feet flat on the ground without causing yourself permanent physical damage, yet you want to sit and comfortably extend, but not fully extend, your legs while pedaling. When straddling the mountain bike with both feet flat on the ground, you should have a minimum one-inch clearance over the horizontal bar, more if most of your time is on rough terrain. Your handlbars should be level with your seat. In this position you should be able to comfortably reach the handlebars. You will be in a generally upright riding position. I tend to ride with a bit more leg extension to avoid leg cramps when pushing hard.

Frames are measured roughly from where the seat post enters the frame to where the pedal cranks attach to the bottom of the bike. A small frame is seventeen inches, and a large one is twenty-three.

Different bikes have different frame geometry. Frame geometry refers to the relationship of the seat (seat angle) and the front fork (head angle) to the top frame tube, the wheelbase length, and the distance between the rear sprocket and the chainring (chainstay length). Geometry affects fit and performance. Most bikes in our price range have a less aggressive frame geometry. Generally, a long chainstay (over 17 inches), is an indication that the bike you are drooling on is less aggressive. A less aggressive frame is usually more stable, particularly on downhills. It is a good general mountain touring choice. When you see 16.5- to

17-inch chainstays, the bike will generally be more responsive to your movements and more responsive to the terrain. This can be good or bad, depending on your skill level and/or the type of riding you like to do. An aggressive bike climbs better, but it can be squirrely on fast descents. This responsiveness versus downhill stability issue is the same issue you face when buying skis. Not all top mountain bike racers race aggressive frame designs; they decide what is best for them. You need to decide what is best for you.

For most backcountry touring, fit is the most important consideration. Try different frame sizes, adjust the seat and handlebars, and try different makes until you come up with the best combination.

Some bikes are imported with thin, 1.5-inch tires; it has to do with a tariff or something. Get some fat tires on before someone sees you on the bike. You will notice the difference. There are various types of tires available, and you can get away with a general purpose tire, but as you ride more, do rougher routes, and want better performance, you will want trail type or knobby tires.

What does more money buy in a bike? Sealed bearings for starters. Sealed bearings keep mud, dust, and water out, and the grease in. Without sealed bearings your bike will require additional maintenance. If you plan to ride on dirt roads you'll want this feature.

More expensive mountain bikes usually have more expensive brakes, derailleurs, and gears. Depending on your ability, where you ride, and the way you ride, you may not be able to tell or appreciate the difference. Biopace chainrings and indexing derailleurs are all the rage. Biopace computer designed, kidney shaped chainrings optimize pedaling power. Tests prove they work. I can't tell the difference; but then I'm not a computer. Indexing derailleurs provide a positive click-into-place shift — no more feel-your-way shifting. This is particularly nice in situations where a missed shift means you walk. For instance, when climbing, there is a moment when you still have just enough momentum to sneak in a shift before you overload the chain; if you overshift, in either direction, you may lose your balance or not have the strength to turn the crank.

If you want your new bike to stay new looking, a chip-resistant chrome finish is a nice touch. If you like the exotic, or if you plan to seriously race, you may want a stiff aluminum or alloy frame. A stiffer frame minimizes frame distortion; it gives you a more efficient but harsher ride.

Okay, what do you get if you are willing to pop for a grand, give or take $100 or so? Well, a $1000 bike generally has a hand-built custom frame and top-of-the-line components. For most of us, the performance difference between similarly equipped hand-built versus top-end mass produced frames is in our minds. That doesn't mean I don't want one; it's just that food and shelter have a higher priority right now.

There is no substitute for experience. I can tell you everything there is to know about buying a mountain bike, and it will be useless unless you try a bike out. Don't buy the first bike you see. Go for a few rides. Ask if you can at least give the bike a dirt road trial. You are going to spend a lot of money — be sure to get a bike that fits. As with other equipment, once you have carefully selected your bike, you'll probably want a new one after a season. Time on the bike will tell you what you like, how you like to ride, and where you like to do it.

Get a real mountain bike if you expect to really do mountain biking. Get one that fits if you expect to do it right.

# Precautions, Preparations, and Accessories

*The Basics*

I've had a few flat tires on my ten speed; fewer on my mountain bike. But I won't let Murphy catch me sans tube and tools. The consequences of a flat tire are greater in the boonies than on the open road. Make sure you have a spare tube, a pump, and a set of tire irons — those funny little flat, bent things.

Mountain bike chain links and derailleurs get bent, and brakes and derailleurs need adjustment at all the wrong times. Minor repairs and adjustments can be made with a few simple tools. I carry various box wrenches, a combination screwdriver, a few allen wrenches, a pair of pliers, a chain link extractor, nuts, bolts, and a few other spare parts. Put together a little tool kit and keep it with your bike. A minor repair can save the day atop Schofield Pass.

Prepare for mountain biking as you would prepare for a hike. Take plenty of water; your sweat and the dry Colorado air can lead to dehydration. Water can also help you through a mild case of altitude sickness. Most mountain bikes come with braze-ons for a standard pull-top water bottle. Be sure to bring your water, and resist the temptation to dip into a cool, clear, natural mountain stream. Streams and lakes may carry the micro-organism Giardia lamblia. Giardiasis can at best give you gas and at worst incapacitate you with diarrhea and severe cramps. Boiling, filtering, or treating the water are the only sure bets.

A first-aid kit is a good idea — you are bound to take a spill now and then. Be sure the kit includes a good sunscreen. Don't forget sunglasses, not only at altitude, but anytime it's not dark — sunglasses make good goggles.

I carry a compass. It's fun to locate landmarks on the map, and it's sometimes critical to figure out where you are. Unmarked roads and confusing intersections are common. If you are unfamiliar with an

18

area, make sure you have a map, preferably a topographic map.

Reflectors are mandatory, and a good bike light is a good idea. There are some fine removable AA-size lights around. I have a generator-type light. There are advantages and disadvantages to this style, but I don't want to be caught with dead batteries.

Suit yourself when it comes to kickstands, racks, speedometers, quick-release hubs, seat locators, and other goodies. You will quickly decide how you want to outfit your bike — just make sure you get stuff that won't rattle off or get knocked off. I'm risking it with my generator light.

It took me a while to get into toe clips and straps. Oh ... I knew they worked. I knew how they could increase my pedaling efficiency. I knew that they could keep my feet on the pedals in rough terrain. But what if I crashed into a lake and I couldn't get my feet out? Or what if I rolled over and my bike burst into flames? Well, I only had to slip off the pedals once to be convinced to at least try half clips — kind of a training wheel approach to the real thing. I have since graduated to full toe clips and straps. Once I learned to pull out of a toe clip and loose strap prior to hitting the ground, I was in love with them. If you intend to do serious mountain biking, at least get half clips. Half clips are like full toe clips and straps less the straps.

Think about what you wear. I like to ride in baggy shorts six months out of the year. I have also been caught in baggy shorts on Boreas when it was snowing. Plan for Colorado mountain weather and elevation changes. Don't forget how hot you can get pedaling up and how cold you can get cruising down. Layer your clothes.

Wear a helmet. It's mandatory for sanctioned events for a good reason. Padded gloves cushion shock, and padded pants reduce chafing. There is a good chance that you will be walking some of the time; wear shoes that you can hike in.

I found a tire pressure gauge on the road, so now I check my tire pressure before I ride. I'm not a fanatic about it yet, but 40-60 psi on pavement and 30-40 psi on gravel and dirt does make sense.

With Rocky Mountain summers come Rocky Mountain afternoon thunderstorms — hail, lightning, and driving rain. Start early and pack a poncho. Be prepared for the worst in weather or whatever. On a long ride into the backcountry, make sure you have a way to stay warm, a way to fix your bike, and a way to treat minor injuries.

This is not scientific, but many experienced riders will tell you that 25 miles on a dirt road is as hard as 50 on pavement. Remember this when planning a tour.

Always be sure you know what the trail conditions are before you ride. Snow, mud, or rockslides occasionally block high mountain trails. When in doubt, call the local Forest Service district office.

# Riding Skills

Let's assume that you know how to mount and pedal a bike. If you're just going to ride around town you can stop here. If not, read on.

The best way to learn to ride a mountain bike is to ride a mountain bike. Learning to control a skid or to anticipate a hazard comes with experience — but there are some things I can tell you.

You'll probably get sick of hearing me say it, but ... mountain biking is a lot like skiing. Lesson number one; don't bail out at the first sign of trouble. There are times, like when you are climbing through rubble, when you just have to resist hopping off your bike when your front wheel lifts off the ground. Tipping over backwards might be an object lesson in the importance of weight distribution, but so often you can do it when you think you can't. Remember to keep your weight forward on inclines — lean forward and hunch down over your handlebars when going up. There is a fine line between keeping your front wheel on the ground and still maintaining traction with the rear. If you want to stand up to pedal, then shift up to a higher gear so that you have some crank resistance to help you keep your balance. The problem with standing is that you are more apt to spin your rear wheel. The advantage is that you can generate more climbing power. When standing, crouch forward to keep your front wheel down, and stick your butt out over the bike seat to keep weight on your rear wheel for increased traction. I occasionally slide so far back that I sit on my lunch.

Deceleration with forward weight transfer happens as you fly down one hill and back up another. Grade and speed dictate where you want your weight. For many rides this may never be a consideration. But on really steep hills (really steep!), you will want to be back in the saddle as you hit the incline and slow, and then move to your climbing position.

When approaching a hill, don't shift down too soon. Give yourself a running start and then drop down to a lower gear, but shift to that lower gear while you still have momentum. Shifting while straining to go uphill doesn't work. Your derailleur will only shift gears when it is lightly loaded. If you are climbing and you need to shift to a lower gear, unload your derailleur by pedaling faster for a few seconds to gain momentum, ease up, and then shift.

Cross-gear shifts frequently won't work, and they are hard on your gears and chain. A cross-gear shift is an attempt to run the chain between your small front chainring and one of your smaller rear freewheel sprockets, or vice versa. Sometimes this cannot be avoided, but when you find that your chain just won't climb over a gear, reduce the tension on it by moving the other end to a middle gear.

Raise your seat on long climbs. You really don't have to mess with your seat that much, but in Colorado, where many rides start as two-hour uphill workouts, you should set your seat for full leg extension (a la ten speed). With full leg extension you generate more power at the expense of balance. A real mountain bike comes with a quick-release seatpost lock; no need for a wrench.

Lower your bike seat when making steep descents. This lowers your center of gravity and eliminates that falling-over-forward feeling. It also puts you in a better position to pick your way through rough terrain — as long as you do not have to do much pedaling.

When you ride rough stuff, time your pedal rotations to clear rocks and other obstacles. When going downhill, avoid hitting smaller obstructions by cruising with the pedal cranks parallel to the ground. Catching a pedal hurts.

As you do when skiing moguls, learn to choose a line. Look ahead and pick your way through the obstacles. As you get better and braver you'll want to bounce off a few, but for now take it easy and learn to control your bike.

On to braking — for my money, the single most important skill to learn. Be careful with your front brakes. A quick way to go head over handlebars is to lock your front wheel when going fast or down a hill. Forward weight transfer occurs during braking. When your weight moves over your front wheel, your front brakes become more effective. I practice braking with the front brake. Shift your weight back on your seat as you pull the front brake lever; react to the forward mechanical forces by transferring your weight to the back of the bike. With miles this should be habit — pull, shift, pull, shift.

Watch for loose gravel. On back roads loose gravel is frequently deep gravel. You don't need to avoid it — just be careful in it. Deep, loose gravel, like deep, heavy snow, can throw you forward. Be careful with your front brake and keep your front wheel straight. A little forward weight transfer along with a turned bike in loose gravel and you too can do flying over the handlebar stunts.

When it comes to skiing, you all know about skidding versus carving turns. Back on your bike, brake before the turn, and then let up on the brakes and glide or power through the turn. Avoid skids by avoiding the brakes. Plan ahead for your turn.

Get in the habit of keeping at least your thumb and forefinger wrapped around the handlebar grip when riding in rubble. You can still brake with your remaining fingers. But hitting a rock or rut can jerk the handlebars out of your hands if you don't have a good grip.

Get up off your seat and push off on the pedals when going over bumps. Let your legs absorb the shock. When you can't avoid a rock or a log, or when you don't want to avoid it, learn to transfer your weight to the rear tire, push hard on your pedals, and lift your front wheel up over the obstacle. Then transfer your weight forward and unweight the rear wheel as you complete your hop. Keep your weight off the wheel that is making contact with an obstacle.

It's fun to bounce down a four-wheel-drive trail at twenty miles per hour, but ... you had better know what you are doing. Ride under control. Be alert. Keep a safe distance between riders.

# Very Simple Maintenance and Care

I like to do minor adjustments, replace brake pads, and fix bent things. I leave the tough stuff to a bicycle mechanic. Suit yourself and your pocketbook in this regard.

Something we can all do is to wash our bikes after a muddy ride. Dirt, mud, and dust cause unnecessary drive train wear, encourage squeaks, and contribute to sluggish gear changes. Be careful in the car wash. High-pressure sprays can drive water into your bearings, doing more harm than good. I occasionally use a degreaser when I wash my bike. After a wash, spray your chain, gears, and derailleurs with bike lube.

Bouncing off rocks loosens things. It seems that mountain bike bolts and nuts require constant attention. Be sure to check your headset, brakes, shifters, and spokes before you take a major ride.

# Using the Route Descriptions

For this book, I have defined the Front Range as an area loosely bordered by Denver, Ft. Collins, Grand Lake, Dillon, Fairplay, and Colorado Springs. Select your route from the Front Range route location map (Area Map) or pick it from the Appendix — a tabulation of the same rides by ride rating: easy, moderate, and strenuous.

Each route description has two ratings. The ride rating is a composite rating that takes into account the physical strength and endurance required. It also indirectly takes into account the level of skill needed. The ratings are based on normal route conditions — snow, mud, or water could dramatically change a route.

A more technical ride will generally require more strength and endurance. A beginning or intermediate ride can also be strenuous if there is a long climb.

You can make an easy ride strenuous if you really push it. A strenuous ride can be moderate if you walk the hard parts. Whether you are a beginner or an old pro, don't be afraid of any of the routes — just be aware of what you are getting into and plan accordingly.

Each ride also has a skill level rating: beginning, intermediate, or advanced. I would rate an all-weather gravel road with some ruts and moderate inclines as a beginning tour; no particular mountain biking skills are required. A four-wheel-drive trail with rocks, obstructions, and 40 percent grades would merit an advanced rating. Intermediate is somewhere in between. You'll soon get the hang of it.

Frequently a route will start out easy and beginning only to end up strenuous and advanced. I will point this out so you can decide if you only want to do part of a route. If a large part of a ride is advanced, I will rate it advanced. But if a beginning route has a short advanced section, I may still call the route easy and assume you can walk the hard part.

The ride and skill ratings are quite subjective, and influenced by the weather and how I feel. I have tried to make adjustments. Beginners can be assured that an easy/beginning ride is about as easy as you can get. Trip mileage is approximate; I used a bicycle speedometer/odometer, rounded off the tenths, and attempted to account for a few route diversions. Ride time is just as approximate. Remember, stronger, more skillful bikers will go faster. Ride time means time in the saddle. On a one-way ride, ride time is the time it takes to ride from point A to point B. Lunch, fishing, and wildflower identification time is not included. After a few rides you will be better able to estimate your own time.

At a dinner party in Boulder recently, I met a couple who mentioned that they had just started mountain biking. Without knowing who I was, they said, "Boy, would we like to" — I can't recall if they said choke or strangle — "the guy who wrote this mountain biking guide." My, what a coincidence, it seems that a friend of theirs had a copy of

***Easy/Beginning.*** *Generally flat with occasional easy hills on a smooth, unpaved road surface.*

**27**

*Bicycling the Backcountry.* I listened. Well, as it turns out, these folks took their first ever mountain bike ride on a beginning skill level, 32-mile, moderate/strenuous rated route, on a constant grade, up to over 12,000 feet. The ride had a relatively steep elevation graph, and a four-hour on-the-bike ride time. They didn't bring enough water, and they decided not to bring a lunch. The ride took them over five hours, and they had to work pretty hard. They read "beginning" and thought they understood. Make sure you understand the entire ride description at the beginning of each route and plan accordingly.

Many of these routes are simply one part of a trail/route labyrinth. Frequently a 5-mile ride can be extended into an all-day outing by simply taking other roads in the area. Wherever practical I have selected rides that lead to backcountry ride clusters. Frequently the rating and description of a route are indicative of the immediate area.

**Moderate/
Intermediate.**

*Typically a
mixture of easy
to relatively
harder hills.
Expect
occasional
loose gravel
and ruts.*

Because you will generally be biking on a road, you can change the trip mileage by parking and starting in a different place. But if a route is on a four-wheel-drive road, don't try it in your VW.

Using the Route Descriptions

I have indicated the starting elevation and the highest point on each route. The elevation changes are shown on the elevation/distance graph in the route descriptions. This graph approximates a cross section of the terrain for a given route. Elevations are taken from topographic maps. Unless I was able to pinpoint an exact elevation location, I rounded elevations off.

You should be able to get to a route with the Front Range location map (Area Map), and you should be able to pedal the route with the topographical map and description provided in this book. If you decide to explore an alternative route, or if you want to know more about an area,consider taking a topo map along. I have listed several maps, including the appropriate USGS County Series 1:50 000-scale topographic map,

**Strenuous/ Advanced.**

*A major part of the ride is on a steep, rocky, and rutted road.*

and the Trails Illustrated Colorado Series map for each
ride. These maps are generally more useful for
bicycling because they cover considerably more area
than a single USGS 1:24 000-scale 7.5-minute quad-
rangle map. However, I have also listed the USGS
7.5-minute quads for you diehards who have them
tucked away in your basement and just want to take
a peek. Personally, I like Trails Illustrated maps; they
are waterproof, tearproof, and they pack well. I like
them so much, in fact, that my wife and I bought the
company. They can be cross referenced with USGS
quads and picked up at your favorite sports equipment
store.

A topo map describes terrain in intervals as shown
by contour lines. Each line represents a given altitude.
The darker index lines are marked with the altitude.
The lighter intermediate lines represent in-between
altitude gradations. A typical topographic map may
have forty- or eighty-foot contour intervals — it is
noted on the map. At a glance, close index lines mean
steep grades.

I describe inclines in terms of percent grade rather
than in degrees. Percent grade is the method of expres-
sing vertical drop that you usually see on ski slopes
and highways. Moguls typically start to form on a 40
percent slope; I think you get the idea.

I have described these routes as they were in 1986
and 1987. Some things may have changed. It is your
responsibility to be aware of change, and it is your
responsibility to be prepared for a given mountain
bike ride.

# Your Duty —
# Preserving the Mystique

It's okay to walk your bike when alone or around other mountain bikers. But *never* walk your bike, unless you are about to tear a quad or collapse a lung, when in view of anyone on or in a motorized off-road vehicle.

"Did you really ride your bike up here?"

"You bet."

"Wow."

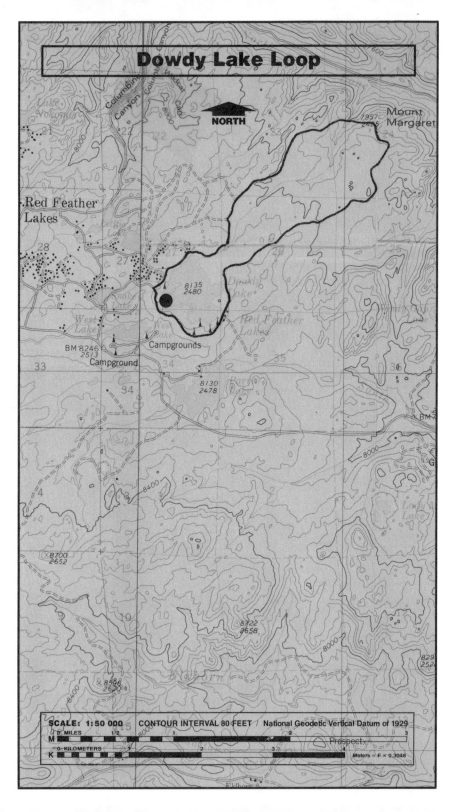

# Dowdy Lake Loop

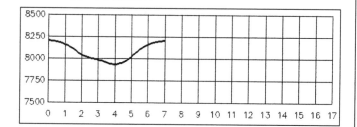

*Ride rating*
**Moderate**

*Skill level*
**Intermediate**

*Round trip*
**7.0 miles**

*Approximate ride time*
**2.0 hours**

*Starting elevation*
**8200 feet**

*Highest point*
**8200 feet**

*Maps*
**Roosevelt National Forest**
**USGS 7.5-minute Red Feather Lakes**
**USGS 1:50 000-scale Larimer County - 2**
**Trails Illustrated #111 Red Feather Lakes**

The Red Feather Lakes area is known for good fishing. But for me, the main attraction is mountain biking — the ride possibilities seem endless. There is a wide range of routes in the area, many on closed roads. The Red Feather Ranger Station has a list of roads that are closed to motorized vehicles. There are several campgrounds with facilities, and, once in the National Forest, many places to just pitch a tent.

Most of this ride is on a restricted road closed to motorized vehicles. On a weekend ride, we only saw one other mountain biker — don't tell your friends

about this ride. Oh, by the way, the other rider had
a flat tire — no spare tube or patch kit. It was a
long walk. Be sure to read the chapter "Precautions,
Preparations, and Accessories."

Red Feather Lakes is located over 20 miles west of
Fort Collins. From Fort Collins take U.S. Hwy. 287
north to Livermore. Turn left and head west on Red
Feather Lakes Road. At Red Feather Lakes, turn right
on Dowdy Drive, pass the ranger station, and take
Forest Route 218 to the right. Turn right at the
Roosevelt National Forest Recreational Area sign and
park in the boat ramp parking lot. You can also park
your car at Red Feather Lakes and pedal from there
to here — it's not very far.

From the parking lot, turn left on Dowdy Drive
and pedal toward the campground on an all-weather
gravel road. Pedal past the campground guardhouse,
past the campground, and up to a locked gate at 1.3
miles. The road is closed to motorized vehicles beyond
this point. Head right and enter the restricted area
through the opening about 20 yards from the locked
gate. At this point, the road is a pretty good dirt road
that soon becomes a good two-pather with a 5-10
percent incline grade.

There is an easy decline to a gate at 1.7 miles.
Open the gate, close it behind you, and continue to a
four-road intersection at 2.6 miles. Such a great
quandary. Well, we'll head straight ahead, toward Mt.
Margarete. Stay on the obvious main road at 2.8 miles.
The road is a series of flat spots and easy ups and
downs. There is a meadow at 3.2 miles. There is a
little wetland area to the left. And there is a fork in
the road — head left. Believe it or not, this is a road.
It is overgrown for the next 30 yards or so, so just
curl around the water and pedal up to the Firewood
Area D sign at 3.5 miles. As you might expect, the
area is patrolled by redwing blackbirds. Back where I
come from, marauding redwing blackbirds go with
worm fishing and wool baseball caps.

The road soon starts to look like a road as you pedal up a moderate incline to a fine northwesterly view at 3.8 miles. Cruise over some easy ups and downs to an intersection at 4.2 miles. Turn right, and at 4.3 miles head down a steep, 20-30 percent 75-yard decline, and then push it up a similarly steep incline. At 4.4 miles there is a road to the left — don't turn; go straight and down to a little creek. It's July, and oh, how the columbines are out.

Head up an easy incline and into a pretty meadow at 4.8 miles. Grass again takes over the road — follow the double worn paths as another road joins in at 4.9 miles. You are headed southwest at 5.1 miles. The road is better. Ponderosa pine predominates, and there are many wildflowers in this open and flat section.

There is a side road to the right at 5.2 miles; stay on the road you are on and bear to the left. There is another side road, to the left, at 5.5 miles; keep to the right. There is a gate at 5.8 miles; go through it.

*Dowdy Lake loop ride*

There are now houses and people and dogs. Take the fork to the right at 5.9 miles. This is Letitia Trail — it's marked. Stay on Letitia Trail to Letitia Circle at 6.2 miles, turn left, continue to Dowdy Drive, and finally pedal around the lake to your vehicle at 7.0 miles. On the shore with a coachman on the line, I hooked two small rainbows.

# Manhattan Road to Swamp Creek

**2**

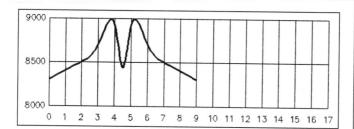

*Ride rating*
**Moderate**
*Skill level*
**Intermediate**
*Round trip*
**9.2 miles**
*Approximate ride time*
**2.0 hours**
*Starting elevation*
**8300 feet**
*Highest point*
**9000 feet**
*Maps*
**Roosevelt National Forest**
**USGS 7.5-minute Red Feather Lakes, Rustic**
**USGS 1:50 000-scale Larimer County · 1**
**Trails Illustrated #111 Red Feather Lakes,**
**#112 Poudre River**

This route is south of Red Feather Lakes. The first few miles are easy. If you have the time, you can ride all the way to Glen Echo and Rustic down in the Poudre Canyon. There is a range of good camping in the area, from campgrounds with facilities to primitive campsites.

Cabins first appeared here in the early 1870s. The resort town of Red Feather Lakes was established in 1923 and was named after a legendary Cherokee Indian chief. The early resort promoters produced a

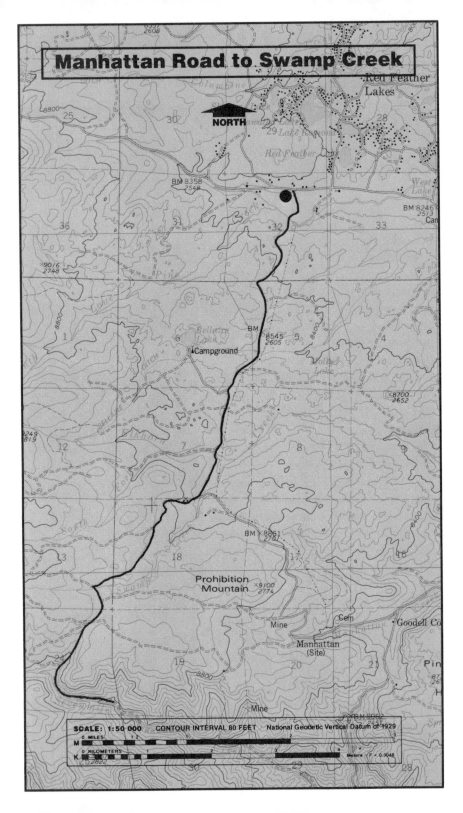

# Manhattan Road to Swamp Creek

film in which Chief Red Feather graciously says, "I give you my land." Thanks, Chief.

Red Feather Lakes is located over 20 miles west of Fort Collins. From Fort Collins take U.S. Hwy. 287 north to Livermore. Turn left and head west on Red Feather Lakes Road. You can park at Red Feather Lakes, or you can park in the wide spot at the intersection of Red Feather Lakes Road and Manhattan Road, the first left west of town. This description assumes the latter.

Head south on Manhattan Road, an all-weather, gravel, wide, rolling, and well-traveled road. On a Sunday ride, we saw some traffic in the beginning, not a lot, but enough to alert us that there could be more. But later, the undisturbed raindrop marks on the road confirmed that we were the first folks along in some time.

The first part of this ride consists of a series of easy ups and downs. The predominant tree is ponderosa pine. Ponderosa pine grows at elevations ranging from 6000 to 9500 feet. They may exceed 300 years of age. They do not like the shade, so you

*Campsite near Crown Point*

will frequently see them standing alone.

Back on the road, the Bellaire Campground is at 2.1 miles. Bellaire Lake is considered a good lake for rainbow trout. Bald Mountain Road, Forest Route 517, is at 2.2 miles. This four-wheel-drive road goes up to around 11,000 feet — you may wish to explore it later. For now continue on Manhattan Road to a cattle guard and Forest Route 198, Swamp Creek Road, at 2.7 miles. Turn right and head up Swamp Creek Road.

Thick stands of lodgepole pine replace the ponderosa pine as you approach 9000 feet. At 3.3 miles there is a road to the right and a bridge to the left. Head left, take the bridge, and cross Swamp Creek. The road is still in pretty good shape. That's good, because you are now starting to have more ups than downs, with some inclines in the 20-25 percent range. There are several good campsites along the road. We saw elk tracks all along this section of the road.

To prevent road erosion, there are water bars all along the way. Water bars look like big speed bumps. As a result, they not only redirect water but they slow down and discourage motorized traffic. Water bars can add a little excitement to your bike ride.

Stands of aspen start to appear at 3.5 miles. Stay on the main road at 3.6 miles and bend to the right. Ride the easy roller coaster up and down to the 30 percent incline that takes you to the end at 4.6 miles. There is more to ride if you want — if you have a good map you can get down to Rustic. On this day, this was simply a convenient place to turn around.

# Dadd Gulch Loop

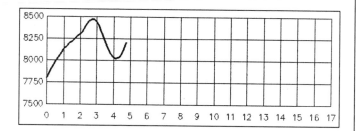

## 3

*Ride rating*
**Moderate/Strenuous**

*Skill level*
**Intermediate/Advanced**

*Round trip*
**4.8 miles**

*Approximate ride time*
**2.0 hours**

*Starting elevation*
**7800 feet**

*Highest point*
**8500 feet**

*Maps*
**Roosevelt National Forest**
**USGS 7.5-minute Rustic**
**USGS 1:50 000-scale Larimer County - 2**
**Trails Illustrated #112 Poudre River**

Dadd Gulch is just one of many good Poudre Canyon rides. There are several side roads along this route; try a few if you have time. This is my kind of ride — picturesque, varied, and challenging. Don't be afraid to try this one; you can walk the hard parts. We made this a family outing; even took the dog.

The Poudre Canyon is a popular place. There are several campgrounds in the area. The Cache La Poudre River flows from Rocky Mountain National Park. The name has something to do with where the French liked to hide their gunpowder. The Poudre is one of

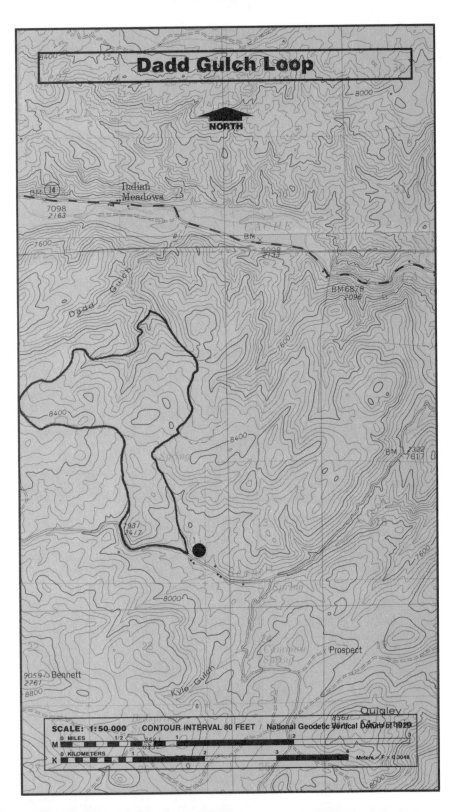

# Dadd Gulch Loop

NORTH

SCALE: 1:50 000   CONTOUR INTERVAL 80 FEET / National Geodetic Vertical Datum of 1929

the state's best-known trout streams. Dadd Gulch is between the Cache La Poudre and Bennett Creek, a tributary.

From Fort Collins take U.S. Hwy. 287 north, and then Colorado Hwy. 14 west and up the Poudre Canyon. There is a bridge over the Cache La Poudre about 5 miles east of Glen Echo. This is Forest Route 131; take it, cross over the river, and after a few miles turn right onto Forest Route 139, Crown Point Road. In about a mile, cross over a cattle guard and park in the wide spot along the road. The road you want is directly to the right, on the north side of Crown Point Road.

This ride is somewhat complex because of the constant 15-20 percent incline, the loose gravel, and the ruts. It's not that bad, but you'll either learn how to maintain traction or you'll walk. There are some water bars along the way. These are designed to prevent road erosion. They are also a good place to practice jumps and such.

There is a side road at 0.3 miles; stay on the obvious main road and continue up to a very steep

*Dadd Gulch*

(try 50 percent in places) incline at 0.6 miles. It's only about 50 yards long; you may want to try it a few times just for fun. There is a respite from the grade at the top, soon followed by more climbing. Make sure you turn around and take a gander at the Mummy Range.

There is a meadow at 1.0 miles. In July we saw changing aspen, as well as harebell, flax, sego lily, vetch, yarrow, Indian paint brush, Indian blanket, showy daisy, sticky geranium, penstemon, and ... I'm sure glad Mary was along — to me they're all just pretty flowers. Ponderosa pine dots the southern slope. At 1.4 miles there is a bit of a road to the right; stay on the main road. Head down a moderate and then steep, tricky descent at 1.7 miles. It's uphill again (20-30 percent) at 1.9 miles, followed by a series of ups and downs.

I'm not sure who was the attraction, but the buzzards were flying unnervingly close. I mean close. So close that they provided shade. Anyhow, there is an intersection with a better road at 2.5 miles; turn left and head down an easy decline. Stay on the main road all along this stretch and pedal up to the gate at 3.1 miles. Ride through the gate and turn left onto Forest Route 259. At 3.9 miles Forest Route 259 intersects Forest Route 139. Make a left and head back to the start.

# Crown Point Road

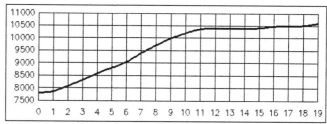

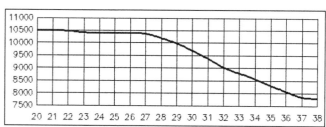

## 4

*Ride rating*

**Moderate**

*Skill level*

**Beginning**

*Round trip*

**38.4 miles**

*Approximate ride time*

**7.0 hours**

*Starting elevation*

**7800 feet**

*Highest point*

**10,600 feet**

*Maps*

**Roosevelt National Forest**

**USGS 7.5-minute Rustic, Kinnikinik**

**USGS 1:50 000-scale Larimer County - 1, 2, & 3**

**Trails Illustrated #112 Poudre River**

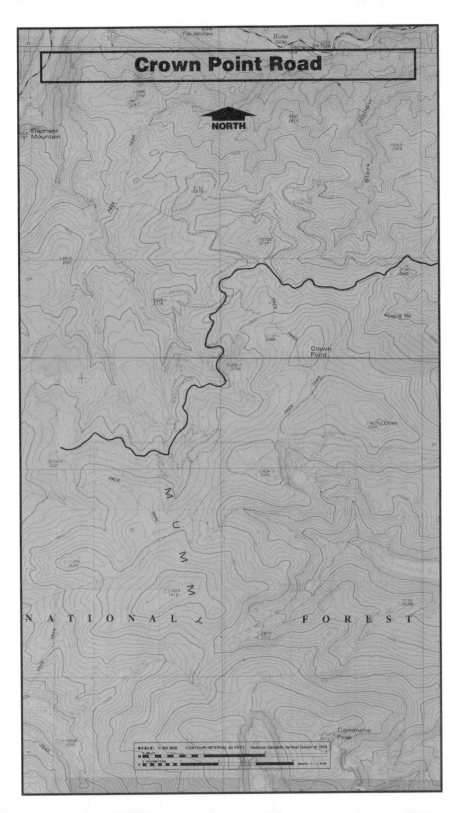
# Crown Point Road

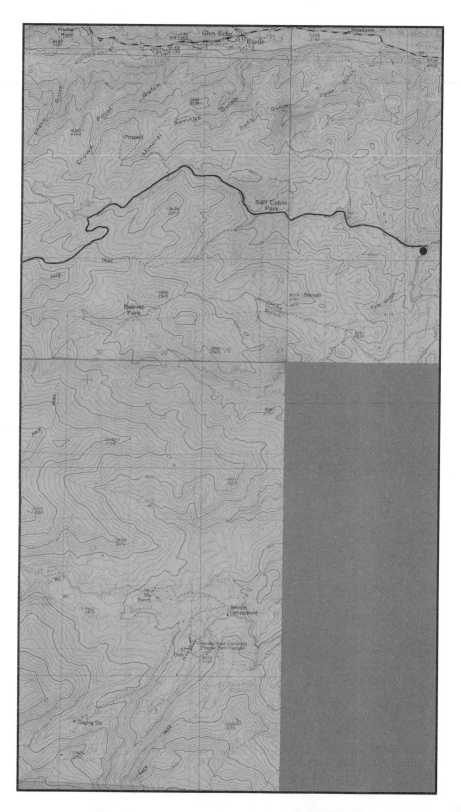

**Crown Point Road**

Crown Point Road cuts through the northern end of the Mummy Range. It leads to several Comanche Peak Wilderness trailheads — expect some traffic. There are campsites in the area. Combine Crown Point Road with the Dadd Gulch Loop route for a Poudre Canyon weekend.

The Mummy in Mummy Range is because someone thought the range looked like a reclining mummy. The Arapaho Indians called these mountains the White Owls. The high Mummies, to the south, are within Rocky Mountain National Park.

From Fort Collins take U.S. Hwy. 287 north, and then Colorado Hwy. 14 west and up the Poudre Canyon. There is a bridge over the Cache La Poudre about 5 miles east of Glen Echo. This is Forest Route 131; take it, cross over the river, and after a few miles turn right onto Forest Route 139, Crown Point Road. Park along the side of the road and start pedaling up Crown Point Road. Now I realize that I am being a little glib here; you know, just hop on your bike and pedal, uphill, for the next 20 miles or so and then head back. Oh, and don't forget that 40 miles on a gravel road is like 80 on pavement. Well, this really is a moderate and beginning ride. But, it's the length that might get you into trouble if you are not in the best of shape. Another approach to this ride is to drive to the end and pedal around on top. You will have no trouble finding a few hours of good riding. Don't worry, your VW can handle the road. I'll describe this route from the beginning, but remember, you have an option.

This ride starts out on an easy-riding, all-weather gravel road. At first it passes by private property. Later there are campsites along the way. Spruce, aspen, and Douglas fir are the predominant trees.

The easy climb gets a bit harder at 2.3 miles. There is a meadow at 2.7 miles. There is a side road at 3.1 miles, and another at 3.2 miles — you can extend this ride by exploring them. For this ride description it's onward and upward on the main road. There are side roads all along the way; you won't need them as reference points — the route is obvious.

It's still all uphill at 5.1 miles. The road is the same. Lodgepole pine has replaced the earlier mix. Lodgepole pine ranges from less than 8000 feet above sea level in warm, dry areas to cool, high elevations exceeding 10,500 feet. It typically occurs as a pure, dense stand. One look at the straight trunk tells you how the lodgepole got its name.

The road conditions remain pretty constant over the next few miles. The long climb is over at 9.1 miles. Here at over 10,000 feet you are in the sub-alpine life zone, the spruce-fir ecosystem. Distant waves of whitecapped mountains mark the boundary between earth and sky as you move along this sometimes flat, sometimes descending road. The Browns Lake trailhead is at 11.8 miles. Crown Point (11,400 feet) is to the left.

You're climbing again at 12.8 miles — nothing serious. The remainder of the ride is a roller coaster of easy ups and downs. There is a creek at 15.5 miles, another at 17.2 miles, and another at 18 miles. The road ends in a parking area, at the Zimmerman and Crown Point trailheads, at 19.2 miles.

*Crown Point Road*

*Crown Point Road*

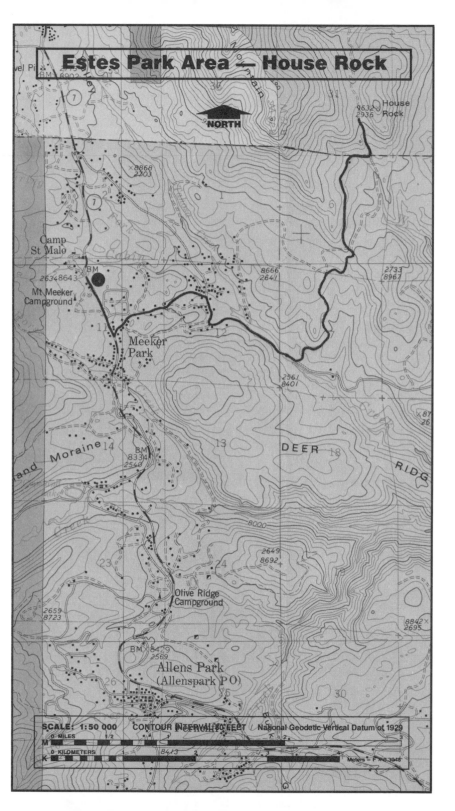

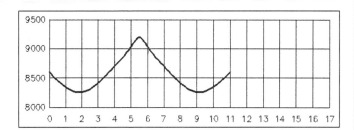

Ride rating

**Strenuous**

Skill level

**Intermediate**

Round trip

**11.0 miles**

Approximate ride time

**3.0 hours**

Starting elevation

**8600 feet**

Highest point

**9300 feet**

Maps

**Roosevelt National Forest**

**USGS 7.5-minute Allens Park, Raymond,**

**Panorama Peak**

**USGS 1:50 000-scale Boulder County,**

**Larimer County - 4**

**Trails Illustrated #200 Rocky Mountain National Park**

There are several good mountain biking routes in the Estes Park area. Estes Park is 36 miles northwest of Boulder on U.S. Hwy. 36. For information about other routes, stop in at one of the local bike shops, or pick up a copy of *Bicycling the Backcountry*.

Estes Park, like Aspen, Crested Butte, and Telluride, is in the right place, only for different reasons. There is no gold or silver or coal here; Estes Park has been a tourist town almost from the start.

Joel Estes plunked himself down in the valley in 1859. Colorado's first dude ranch followed in the 1870s. Estes Park is the gateway to Rocky Mountain National Park. Estes Park is breathtaking — period.

Park and unload in the Meeker Park National Forest picnic ground 8 miles south of Estes Park on Colorado Hwy. 7. Pedal less than a mile south on 7 to Cabin Creek Road, Boulder County Hwy. 82, and head east, left, on an all-weather gravel road. You will ride through a private residential area and then up to an unmarked intersection where you turn right and continue east on 82 along Cabin Creek.

After less than 3 miles there is a sign for House Rock, Estes Park, and Pierson Park. Follow the arrows left and head up and north. You will quickly enter the Roosevelt National Forest. From this point the route gets tougher, starting with a 30 percent grade as you start up the road. It's pretty much a continuous climb from here. You will pick up 1300 feet over the next 3 miles.

The road is a four-wheel-drive road with ruts, rocks, and loose stones. The higher you go the worse it gets. There are some good camping spots along the road, and to the west, a view of Longs Peak that will knock your socks off.

After 4 miles you are up around 9000 feet and still climbing. To the south is a view of Longs Peak (14,256 feet) and Mt. Meeker (13,911 feet). These mountains were landmarks — lighthouses for the prairie schooners. These mountains simply jut out of the plains. Longs Peak is the northernmost fourteener in the Rocky Mountains. Major Stephen D. Long led an expedition into Colorado in 1819 and "discovered" his peak the following year. Longs Peak is a classic climb. The Diamond, the sheer, east face of Longs Peak, is often mentioned along with the San Juan's Lizard Head as *the* Colorado climbs.

Mt. Meeker, Meeker Park, Meeker Ridge, and the town of Meeker are all named after Nathan C. Meeker, one of the founders of Greeley. In 1879, while an agent at the White River Ute Indian Agency, Meeker and the other agency employees were massacred by Indians.

Back on the road again, at 4.5 miles there is a Pierson Park sign. Make a left and go north on Pierson Park Road. In about a mile you will come to a gate straight ahead and House Rock to the right. This is the turnaround point for this tour. If you are still game, open the gate and continue to Pierson Park. Please close the gate after you go through. The road gets quite rough and the descent is quite steep. From this point it is 3 miles to Pierson Park, and 7 to Estes Park.

*Estes Park Area — House Rock*

*Longs Peak*

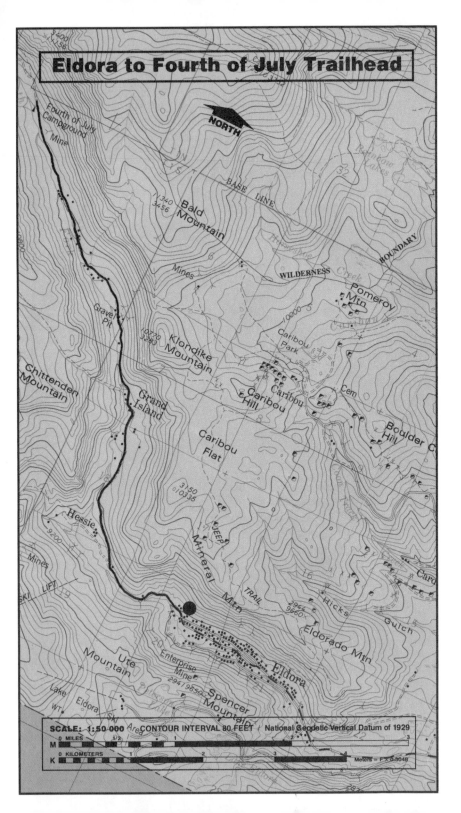

# Eldora to Fourth of July Trailhead

NORTH

Fourth of July
Campground
Mine

Bald
Mountain

BASE LINE

Mines

WILDERNESS

BOUNDARY

Pomeroy
Mtn

Gravel
Pit

Klondike
Mountain

Caribou
Park

Chittenden
Mountain

Grand
Island

Caribou
Hill

Caribou

Cem

Boulder
Hill

Caribou
Flat

Hessie

JEEP

Mineral
Mtn

TRAIL

Hicks

Gulch

Caro

SKI LIFT

Eldorado Mtn

Ute
Mountain

Enterprise
Mine
2941/9650

Eldora

Lake
Eldora

WT

SKI Area

Spencer
Mountain

SCALE: 1:50 000   CONTOUR INTERVAL 80 FEET / National Geodetic Vertical Datum of 1929

0 MILES   1/2   1   2   3
M

0 KILOMETERS   1   2   3   4
K

Meters = F X 0.3048

# Eldora to Fourth of July Trailhead

**6**

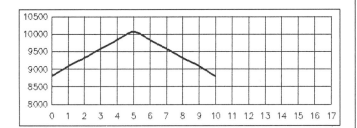

*Ride rating*
**Moderate/Strenuous**
*Skill level*
**Intermediate**
*Round trip*
**10.0 miles**
*Approximate ride time*
**2.5 hours**
*Starting elevation*
**8800 feet**
*Highest point*
**10,200 feet**
*Maps*
**Roosevelt National Forest**
**USGS 7.5-minute East Portal, Nederland**
**USGS 1:50 000-scale Boulder**
**Trails Illustrated #103 Rollins Pass**

There are many places to ride a mountain bike in Boulder County. Pick up a map or stop in and visit one of the local mountain bike dealers to find out where. Eldora is a fun place to just pedal around. There are a few explorable four-wheel-drive roads in the area, and this route is a fairly civilized ride on an all-weather road. Your VW can make it.

Eldora is short for Eldorado. When the early settlers tried to get a post office for their Eldorado, they were told that the folks down the way had already claimed Eldorado for Eldorado Springs. The name tells it all — these mountains are replete with mines, ghosts, and old dreams. The town southeast of Eldora was once known as Brownsville, then known as Middle Border, then Tungsten Town, before the Dutch owners of the Caribou silver mines named it Nederland, meaning "low land," which at first glance sounds a bit silly.

Nederland is west of Boulder and south of Ward at the intersection of Colorado Hwy. 119 and Colorado Hwy. 72. Eldora is just southwest of Nederland; follow the signs. Drive to the west end of Eldora to where the pavement turns to gravel. This is Forest Route 107. Park along the side of the road, hop on your bike, and continue up the road. You are soon climbing a 10 percent incline, and the road quickly gets rougher than it was. It's not bad — just rougher than it was. Expect a fair amount of traffic; this is a popular access road to the Indian Peaks Wilderness Area. The Indian Peaks tag comes from the nearby mountains called Paiute, Pawnee, Shoshoni, Apache, Navajo, and Arapaho.

Hessie Road is at 0.8 miles; stay to the right and continue on Forest Route 107, Fourth of July Road. The Lake Eldora Ski Area is at 1.0 miles. It's not always easy to differentiate private land from public land, so play it safe and stay on the main road.

Aspen and lodgepole pine dominate the forest at this elevation. These two trees can quickly take over disturbed mountain forest sites. In an area clear cut or cleared by fire, you can expect to see aspen or lodgepole, or both. As these invaders create shade, they limit their own reproduction. Climax species, Douglas fir in the montane life zone and Engelmann spruce and subalpine fir in the higher subalpine life zone, thrive in the shade and slowly supplant the aspen and lodgepole to create a climax forest.

In August the wildflowers were a treat. We saw Indian paintbrush, yarrow, showy daisies, fireweed, monkshood, harebells, and yellow paintbrush. The incline grade is up to 10-15 percent at 2.5 miles, and then it's on to a roller coaster of ups and downs for the next couple of miles. The creek on the left side of the road is the North Fork of the Middle Boulder.

The view opens up as you approach tree line. Buckingham Campground is at 5.0 miles. This is the end. Have a snack and head back to Eldora.

Fourth of July Road

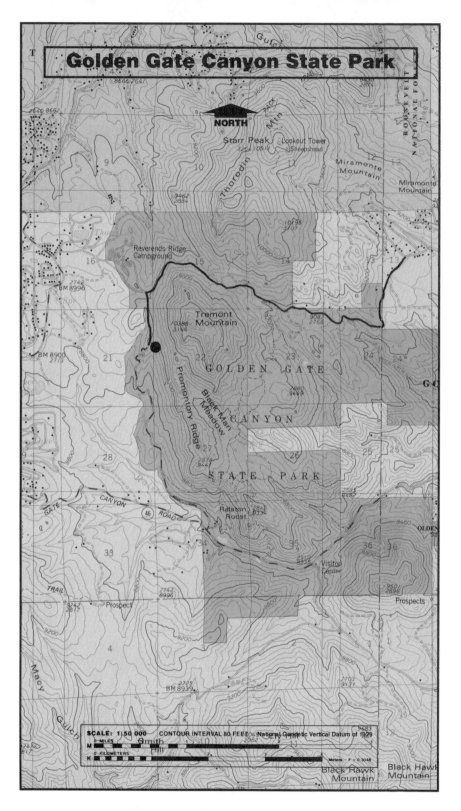

# Golden Gate Canyon State Park

**NORTH**

SCALE: 1:50 000   CONTOUR INTERVAL 80 FEET   National Geodetic Vertical Datum of 1929

# Golden Gate Canyon State Park

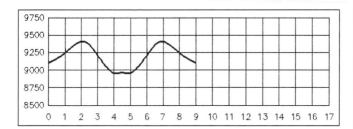

*Ride rating*
**Moderate**
*Skill level*
**Beginning/Intermediate**
*Round trip*
**9.0 miles**
*Approximate ride time*
**2.25 hours**
*Starting elevation*
**9100 feet**
*Highest point*
**9400 feet**
*Maps*
**Arapaho National Forest**
**USGS 7.5-minute Black Hawk, Ralston Buttes**
**USGS 1:50 000-scale Gilpin County,**
**Jefferson County - 1**

September 1987. The yellow trees and white peaks are simply breathtaking. The sun is bright and hot. The air is cold and clean. The aura is electric; it's intense. Let me tell you ... it beats going to work. Is it Tuesday? Well then, you have my permission to take the afternoon off. Why don't you go into the mountains. This is a good place to just go and ride. There are some paved roads in the park, and there is gravel. There are plenty of places to camp, and Golden Gate Canyon State Park is only 16 miles northwest of Golden. You can get up here from the east out of

Boulder and Golden; I chose to enjoy the ride on Colorado Hwy. 119 and enter at the northwest end of the park.

This ride runs across the northern part of the park. You can keep going, get into Coal Creek Canyon, and cruise all the way down to Colorado Hwy. 93. You can do it in reverse and pedal up from the flatlands if you have the energy.

Trappers traveled these mountain meadows in the early 1800s. The beavers that survived owed their skins to the European fashion industry — beaver hats were in and then they were out. There is no gold in Golden Gate Canyon State Park; it was the early gateway to Cental City and Blackhawk where there is gold. Fortune seekers took Golden Gate Road through the park and down to those once teeming goldtown camps in Clear Creek Canyon.

Almost all of this route is on one map; you can get away with using either the Black Hawk or the Gilpin County map; however, the standard park issue, this book, or your sense of direction will probably work just fine. To get there take Colorado Hwy. 119 from Nederland toward Central City. Follow the Golden Gate Canyon State Park sign and head left and east toward the park. Follow the signs to the park entrance. This is a fee area — three bucks in 1987. It's worth it.

Turn to the right at the fee station and information board and drive a short distance to a parking area on the left side of the road. Start pedaling back the way you came. The road is a bit of a roller coaster, but it's paved and easy to ride. At 0.5 miles you are back at the fee station. Turn right and head up a moderate incline on all-weather, gravel Gap Road.

Panorama Point is at 1.0 miles. There is a spectacular 100-mile view of Rocky Mountain National Park, the Continental Divide, and the Front Range. You can see Longs Peak (14,256 feet), and there is a super angle on South Arapaho Peak (13,397 feet). Back on the road again, things are getting a bit rougher as you climb a 15-20 percent incline. The lodgepole pine and aspen start to give way to the Engelmann spruce and subalpine fir as you make the transition from montane to subalpine life zone.

Things start to level off around 1.6 miles, and you start down a moderate decline at 1.8 miles. The Lazy Squaw Ranch is at 2.1 miles. The road is bumpy, but not bad, as you pedal over a series of moderate ups and downs with more downs than ups. The Aspen Meadow Campground turnoff is at 2.4 miles; stay on the main road, continue ahead, and then head down a fairly steep decline to the Rifleman Phillips Group Campground at 3.3 miles. Now don't worry about the return. The road is in good shape; you should be able to keep it in low gear and easily make it back up. There are a few explorable side roads along the way.

The road is a series of ups and downs to the park boundary at 4.0 miles. From here continue through a meadow and to the intersection of Gap and Dowdle. This is a good place to turn around. You can keep going if you want; but this is where I end.

*Golden Gate Canyon*

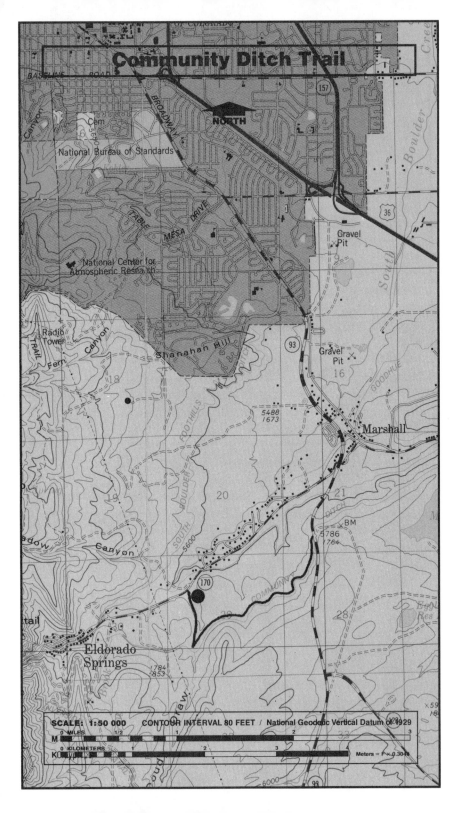
# Community Ditch Trail

# Community Ditch Trail

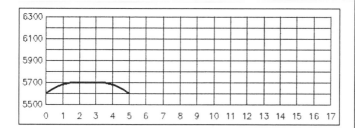

## 8

Ride rating

**Easy**

Skill level

**Beginning**

Round trip

**5.0 miles**

Approximate ride time

**1.0 hour**

Starting elevation

**5600 feet**

Highest point

**5700 feet**

Maps

**USGS 7.5-minute Eldorado Springs, Louisville**
**USGS 1:50 000-scale Boulder County**

This is a good after-supper ride; it's short and easy, the Flatirons vista is grand, and it's much nicer than its name suggests. There are no motorized vehicles on this route. The Community Ditch Trail is part of the Boulder Open Space system. It is located south of Boulder on Colorado Hwy. 170. Oh yes, mountain bikes are legal on this trail. On an early Sunday evening ride, we only encountered a couple of other trail users. But expect to share this route with horses, hikers, and dogs. Be courteous.

The Flatirons dominate the view. The Flatirons are Boulder. They are striking. At once they are bold, threatening, and paternal. It's like they were frozen in mid-flight while leaping out of the ground. They are not meek foothills. They are a bold precursor of things to come — the high Rockies. The Flatirons, along with the rocks at Red Rocks, are composed of sandstone and conglomerate — erosion from the Ancestral Rocky Mountains. The Front Range uplift caused the sediment from the original Rockies to tilt steeply against the rising Front Range. This powerful action produced the distinctive, west-pointing rock formations we call the Flatirons, the Dakota Hogback, and Red Rocks.

To get to the Community Ditch, take Colorado Hwy. 93 to Colorado Hwy. 170. Head west and toward Eldorado Springs and Eldorado Canyon. The Community Ditch Trail is on the left, or south, side of the Hwy. 170, just before Eldorado Springs. The trailhead is well marked. Park in the large parking area and start pedaling up the paved path.

There is a picnic area at 0.3 miles. Follow the bike trail sign and head to the left. You're now on a dirt road of sorts. Follow the bike trail signs to the ditch bridge; don't cross, turn left and continue on the road

*Storm over the Flatirons*

along the side of the ditch. The road is a reasonably good two-pather. The terrain is flat. This is a real easy, real enjoyable ride. At around 1.0 miles there is an Open Space gate; continue through the gate and pedal to another gate at 2.5 miles. At this point you can continue up to and over the highway, and then pedal into the Greenbelt Plateau Open Space. However, I don't wish Hwy. 93 on anyone, especially if you have kids along. We turned around at this point, cruised back to the lot, watched the early evening lightning display, and called it a good day.

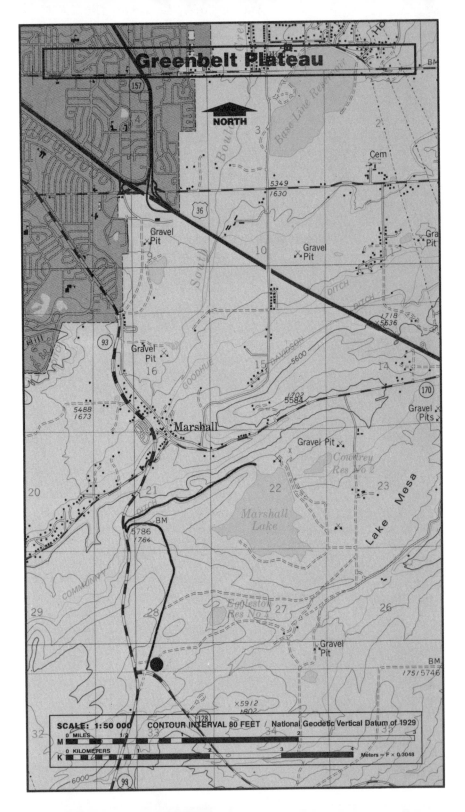

# Greenbelt Plateau

**9**

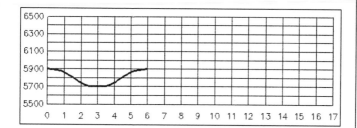

*Ride rating*
**Easy**
*Skill level*
**Beginning**
*Round trip*
**6.2 miles**
*Approximate ride time*
**1.5 hours**
*Starting elevation*
**5900 feet**
*Highest point*
**5900 feet**
*Maps*
**USGS 7.5-minute Louisville**
**USGS 1:50 000-scale Boulder County**

Greenbelt Plateau is part of the Boulder Open Space system. Mountain bikes are allowed on some of the trails — just follow the signs. This is an easy, easy to get to, and enjoyable ride. The Flatirons loom in the west. That's Kansas to the east. This is grassland. You should be able to ride here most of the year. Think of it as a spring tune-up ride. The Greenbelt Plateau trailhead is at the intersection of Colorado Hwy. 93 and Colorado Hwy. 128, between Boulder and Golden, just south of Marshall and north of Rocky Flats.

Marshall is an old coal mining town named for its founder, Joseph Marshall. Rocky Flats manufactures plutonium triggers for atomic bombs. Trigger is sort of a euphemism for the device that is really the heart of the bomb. I don't imagine the Arapaho and Cheyenne would have ceded this land if they had known what we were going to do with it.

We saw a pair of hawks, redtails I guess, soaring so high and then dropping so low and close to us that I could see that they were really hawks. At the same time there was a kid flying a kite, and there was a sailplane soaring overhead.

To get here take Colorado Hwy. 93 to Colorado Hwy. 128, or vice versa. Greenbelt Plateau is on the northeast corner of this intersection. Park in the Open Space parking lot and pedal up the two-path dirt road. The trails are clearly marked. You are likely to encounter hikers; they are generally not dangerous — there is enough room for both of you.

Pedal up a series of easy inclines, with flat spots in between, to a gate at 0.5 miles. Pass through the gate and continue to a crest at 0.9 miles. There is a Boulder view here. That's Marshall Lake to the right. Cruise down to a gate by the side of Hwy. 93 at 1.6 miles. I suspect this gate is locked to keep motorized vehicles out. You can hoist your bike over the gate, or slip it under — it's legal and it's easy.

Turn right, walk a few yards along Hwy. 93, cross over the ditch (you're still on the highway), and head up to the road that runs along the ditch. You can't (shouldn't) miss it. There is another gate at 1.7 miles. It's not locked. Pass through it and continue on this, now a bit rockier, road.

The big trees standing alone are pondeosa pines. They like the sun. There are clumps of Gambel, scrub oak, along the route. Gambel oak is the common oak of the Rocky Mountains. It looks like a shrub and it grows in thickets.

This part of the trail is really the east leg of the Community Ditch Trail — the part on the east side of Hwy. 93. The Community Ditch Trail route described in this book is on the west side of Hwy. 93.

Back on the road, all is pretty much the same, the road is in good shape, the terrain is generally flat, and the surroundings are pleasant as you pedal up to the end, next to Marshall Lake, at 3.1 miles. We just dallied around a bit and then pedaled back to the truck. This was a nice day.

*Greenbelt*
*Plateau*

*The Flatirons*
*from Greenbelt*
*Plateau*

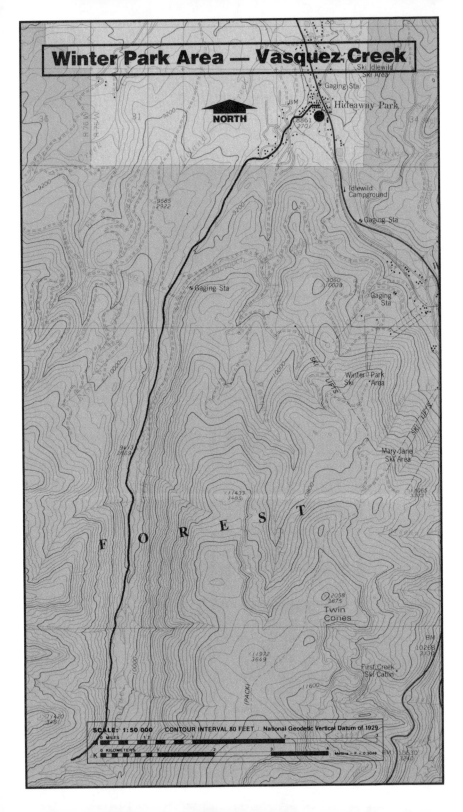

# Winter Park Area — Vasquez Creek

NORTH

SCALE: 1:50 000    CONTOUR INTERVAL 80 FEET    National Geodetic Vertical Datum of 1929

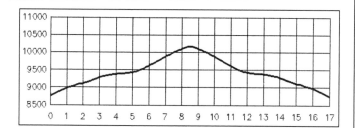

Ride rating

**Easy/Moderate**

Skill level

**Intermediate**

Round trip

**17.0 miles**

Approximate ride time

**3.0 hours**

Starting elevation

**8750 feet**

Highest point

**10,200 feet**

Maps

**Arapaho National Forest**

**USGS 7.5-minute Fraser, Berthoud Pass**

**USGS 1:50 000-scale Grand County - 4**

**Trails Illustrated #103 Rollins Pass**


Winter Park is a fine place to ride; it is a cluster area — a place where you can take a variety of routes. Winter Park's new mountain bike trail system currently has over 150 miles of documented backcountry roads and trails. You can get a system map at one of the local bike shops or from the Winter Park Resort Chamber.

Winter Park started out as a construction camp for the Moffat Tunnel. Back then it was known as West Portal; not such a hot name for a ski resort. (It's also been known as Hideaway Park, as it appears on the

USGS map.) The City of Denver owns the Winter Park Ski Area. Denver mayor Benjamin Stapleton was instrumental in the name change.

Winter park is less than 70 miles from Denver. Take I-70 west to U.S. Hwy. 40. Head up and over Berthoud Pass and down to Winter Park.

Starting in Winter Park, this route takes you up and down Vasquez Creek. The first 5 miles of this route are relatively easy. From the southern side of the main downtown area, go west on Vasquez Road and park in the Winter Park municipal parking garage/lot.

Pedal west on paved Vasquez Road past condos, inns, and private residences. At about 1.0 miles the main paved road turns right. Don't go right; go straight, climb a 10 percent hill, and ride into the Arapaho National Forest. You will find some good camping along the creek. There are a few side roads along the way. Don't be afraid to explore; it's hard to get lost in this valley.

The road is rocky enough to keep your attention, yet easy enough for a beginner. The elevation gain is very moderate all along the first part of the route. Willow-lined Vasquez Creek will be to your left the entire trip up the valley. Forget about fishing; it's not a hot spot. Elephanthead likes cold mountain streams; watch for this nifty wildflower.

At 2.5 miles you are still climbing, but you can probably keep pedaling 8 miles per hour all day. There are many shallow depressions in the road, and they quickly turn into lakes after a rain. If it has rained in the last day, plan on getting wet.

There is a sign at 2.8 miles warning you of a narrow road and blind curves; you are headed the right way. There is some traffic on this road. Be alert.

There is a diversion dam at 4.5 miles and a road over a bridge that will take you back down the other side of the Vasquez. Unless you want to head back, go straight and on to what becomes a four-wheel-drive road.

If you have not already noticed, the forest is now populated with spruce, lodgepole pine, and fir. You are up around 9500 feet and getting into the sub-alpine climate zone.

Around 6.0 miles the road gets rougher and steeper. There is a steady 20 percent grade followed by a short very steep climb. You beginners will probably walk this one. The challenge of a steep hill is to combine strength and endurance with skill. Distribute your weight to keep your front wheel on the ground and your rear wheel biting into the gravel.

Twenty-percent climbs and a rocky road are the norm for the next couple of miles. There is a narrow log bridge over the creek at 6.8 miles. I walked my bike over it. At 7.5 miles, in the summer of 1986, the road was washed out. I carried my bike through the rushing water.

The road is narrow and overgrown until you ride into a large open area at 8.5 miles. This is the end. There is a Continental Divide view. To the south is Vasquez Pass and Stanley Mountain. West of the pass is Vasquez Peak. There is a hiking trail to the left that goes up to Vasquez Pass. A four-wheel-drive road continues for a half mile or so to the right.

*Creek-crossing on Vasquez Road*

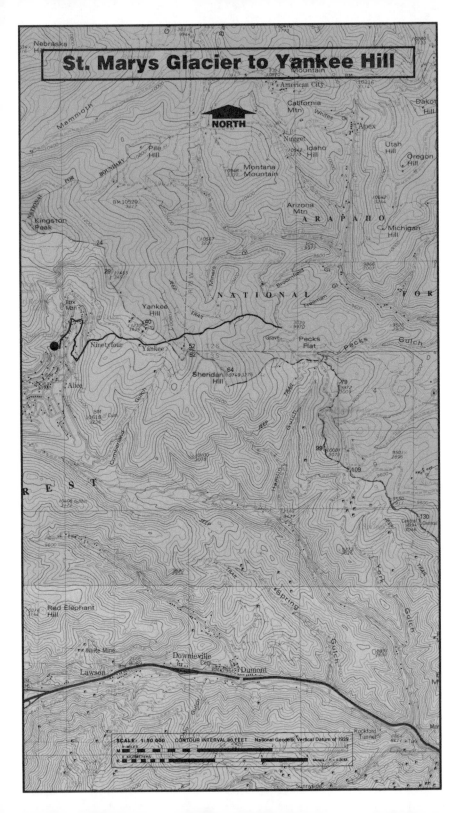

# St. Marys Glacier to Yankee Hill

NORTH

SCALE: 1:50 000    CONTOUR INTERVAL 80 FEET    National Geodetic Vertical Datum of 1929

# St. Marys Glacier to Yankee Hill

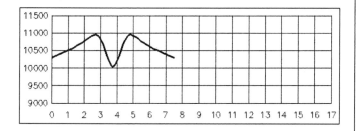

*Ride rating*
> **Strenuous**

*Skill level*
> **Advanced**

*Round trip*
> **7.4 miles**

*Approximate ride time*
> **2.5 hours**

*Starting elevation*
> **10,300 feet**

*Highest point*
> **11,000 feet**

*Maps*
> **Arapaho National Forest**
> **USGS 7.5-minute Empire, Central City**
> **USGS 1:50 000-scale Clear Creek County,**
> **Gilpin County**
> **Trails Illustrated #103 Rollins Pass**

I suspect that it could get crowded up here; but it wasn't on this Thursday — just my friend BD and me, above tree line, enjoying the view and working hard. This is a fine ride. You can ride all the way over to Central City if you have the time and energy. You can shuttle a car. Or you can do as we did and just pedal up to Yankee Hill and back.

Only ghosts remain at Yankee Hill, a once thriving mining boomtown. Named by Yankee sympathizers, Yankee Hill was famed for low-grade ore and bad weather. Gold profit dwindled. Cold weather remained. Guess what happened to the town? There are two other old gold towns in the area — Alice and Ninety Four. Alice was named in honor of the wife of the owner of a mine called the Alice Glory Hole. I'm not sure if Alice appreciated this recognition or not, but it stuck, and the town still stands. Ninety Four was founded in 1894.

From Denver take I-70 to Fall River Road, exit 238, and head toward St. Marys Glacier. In about 8 miles you'll see the St. Marys Glacier Ski Resort. Park in the lot just after the sign on the left. Hop on your bike and continue up a fair incline on the paved road. After about 0.2 miles you will see the sign and trail for St. Marys Lake and St. Marys Glacier — you can hike up there later. Take your skinny skis up there when it snows.

Continue on the paved road into the village area, then go past the lake and to the intersection at around 0.7 miles. Turn right and onto the unpaved road. Lodgepole pine and spruce predominate as you head south and toward Mt. Evans. At 0.9 miles head to the left and down a moderate, rocky decline. At 1.2 miles there is a pond to the right as you start to climb a rocky dirt road. Keep climbing at 1.3 miles; there are a few roads heading down, but just keep climbing — resist the urge. The incline is now over 20 percent and getting steeper. There is a lot of loose gravel and rock on the road.

There is a steep, 40 percent incline to the right at 1.6 miles. This is Forest Route 174. It goes all the way to Central City. Take it. You are pretty good if you can pedal the short distance all the way to the top. At the first crest take the fork to the right — it's marked 175.

Fir, bristlecone pine, and Engelmann spruce take over from the lodgepole as you make the transition from the montane to subalpine life zone. The climb is arduous at 2.1 miles but look behind you — St. Marys

Glacier (the glacier, not the town) is tucked into the side of the mountain — it is a grand site. Note the water bars on the road. These are designed to stem road erosion. At 2.2 miles the grade is 35-40 percent. But then it kind of levels off at 2.3 miles. You can make a hard left at this point, but we are going to follow 175 east and to the right. Note the nifty rock outcroppings to the left.

There is a fork in the road at 2.4 miles; head right and down a moderate decline along the well-marked 175. There are a few side roads that you may want to explore. It's now quite open, so getting lost would be somewhat hard to do. This is Yankee Hill. This is tree line. Krummholz, the wind-ravaged trees that signal your approach to the alpine life zone, now mark the upper limit of the forest — the tree line. Krummholz is German for "crooked wood." At first the windward branches die and the trees begin to look like stiff flags. Then the trees become more deformed and smaller as

*On the road to Central City*

you get higher, until there are no more trees.

The road on the top is in pretty good shape. The ride is certainly easier at this point. The view won't quit — it's a 360-degree lesson in Front Range geography. To the southeast you can identify Squaw Mountain, then Chief Mountain, followed by Mt. Evans (14,264 feet), Grays Peak (14,270 feet), and Torries Peak (14,267 feet). St. Marys Glacier is to the northwest. You are surrounded. Save your lunch till you get to this point.

Bear to the left and stay on Forest Route 175 at 3.1 miles. You are now in a labyrinth as roads head off in all directions — just stay on 175. It is well marked. Keep left at 3.2 miles and right at 3.3 miles. Now, if you want to, start the long decline to Central City. The road is very rocky. Don't be lured into the "I think I'll just keep cruising down this hill" trap; I can guarantee that you will walk part, most, or all of the return to the top. We chose to turn around at 3.7 miles. There is an open ATV playground at this point — you can't miss it. Have fun on the return.

# Hamlin Gulch

**12**

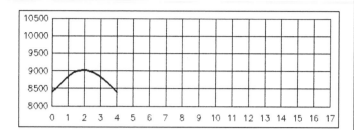

*Ride rating*
> **Moderate**

*Skill level*
> **Intermediate**

*Round trip*
> **4.0 miles**

*Approximate ride time*
> **1.5 hours**

*Starting elevation*
> **8400 feet**

*Highest point*
> **9000 feet**

*Maps*
> **Arapaho National Forest**
> **USGS 7.5-minute Central City**
> **USGS 1:50 000-scale Clear Creek County**
> **Trails Illustrated #103 Rollins Pass**

This is one of those areas where you can ride all day or just ride for an hour or so. Hamlin Gulch is brimming with a variety of mountain bike routes. Don't ask me how, but it's possible to get to Central City from Hamlin Gulch. On a fall weekday we saw a few slow-moving four-wheelers. The terrain forces them to keep their speed down. The aspen trees were grand, and there were some fine Divide views. This is an altogether pleasant ride.

To get there from Denver, take I-70 to Fall River

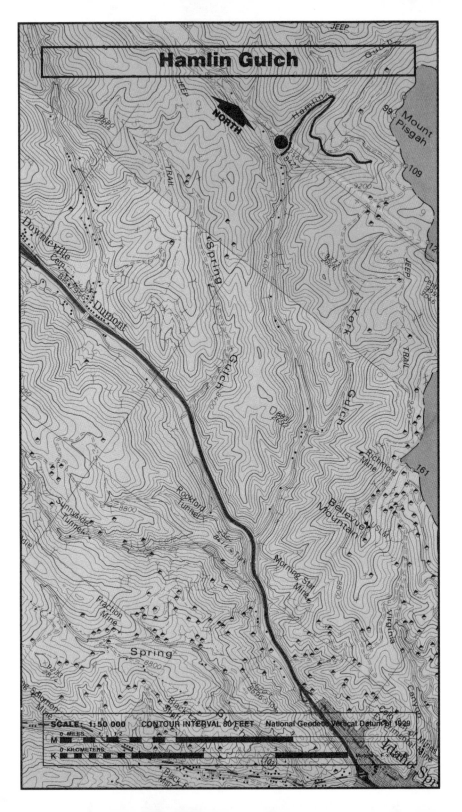

Road, exit 238. Follow the signs to St. Marys Glacier, and in about 3 miles you will see the Hamlin Gulch sign on the right. Park along the side of the road and pedal up a 10-15 percent grade through a nice stand of aspen on a pretty good gravel road. Roses line the road. This is the hardest part of the ride — the road starts to get narrow and a bit rocky as you gain elevation, but it really isn't too bad.

*Hamlin Gulch*

There is a campsite at 0.6 miles, followed by a four-road intersection at 0.8 miles. You can head off in any direction, but for this ride, take the road farthest right and curl back in the general direction you just came from, and of course continue climbing.

There is a nice view opening at 1.0 miles. Lodgepole pine, aspen, Douglas fir, blue spruce, and Gambel oak share the hillside. This is the montane life zone. The road is now a single-lane, four-wheel-drive road. There is a good view of Squaw Mountain, Chief Mountain, and Mt. Evans at 1.3 miles. Stay to the right and on the obvious main road at 1.4 miles.

There is a fork in the road and a marker at 1.5 miles; head right and down. The old road to the right, at 1.8 miles, is marked and closed to motorized

*Hamlin Gulch*

*Hamlin Gulch*

vehicles. This didn't stop a couple of fellows from heading up it. I was quiet — I shouldn't have been. You can explore this road later, but for now continue on the main road over a series of moderate ups and downs, through a grand opening, and to the end at 2.0 miles. There is a water-filled cave at the end of the road. An old mine I presume — this is gold country. Hamlin Gulch is in the Colorado Mineral Belt, a band of faults that runs roughly from Boulder to Silverton. Draw a line on a map between these two cities, and, with the exception of Cripple Creek, you'll see where Colorado gold, silver, lead, copper, molybdenum, and zinc are found. They're all there — Central City, Idaho Springs, Georgetown, Empire, Leadville, Breckenridge, Lake City, Aspen, Ouray, Silverton, and Telluride.

There is a campsite next to the cave at the end. And there is a Mt. Evans view. This is a good place to eat your lunch before heading back to the start.

# Bard Creek Road

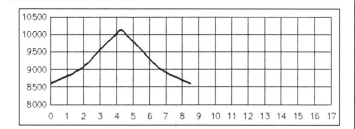

## 13

*Ride rating*
**Strenuous**
*Skill level*
**Advanced**
*Round trip*
**8.5 miles**
*Approximate ride time*
**3.0 hours**
*Starting elevation*
**8600 feet**
*Highest point*
**10,200 feet**
*Maps*
**Arapaho National Forest**
**USGS 7.5-minute Empire, Georgetown**
**USGS 1:50 000-scale Clear Creek County**
**Trails Illustrated #103 Rollins Pass,**
**#104 Loveland Pass**

This is a hard ride. You'll have to be pretty good to do the whole thing on your bike. Don't be afraid to walk parts of it — it's a great hike. Bard Creek Road runs south out of Empire and then heads west and up along Bard Creek. Bard Creek flows into the West Fork of Clear Creek at Empire. Fishing is off-limits along several stretches where the state is attempting to reintroduce the once-native greenback cutthroat trout.

Empire, as in Empire State, was a mining camp

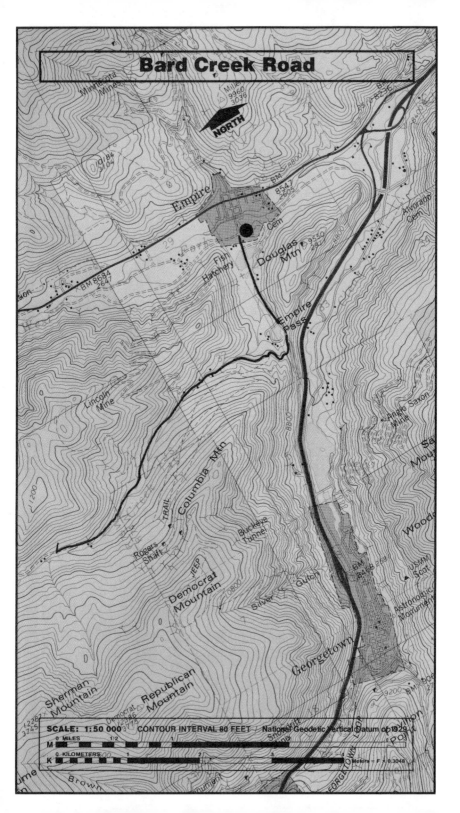

founded in 1860 by four gents from (yes) New York. Local mountains and mines were given names like Lincoln, Sherman, Republican, Democrat, and Columbia as the North fought the South to the east. Low-grade gold ore wasn't enough to keep the population from migrating up the canyon when silver was found at Georgetown; but the allure of a grand historic inn and a good sweet shop may entice you to dawdle today.

*Bard Creek Road*

From Denver take I-70 west. Exit on U.S. Hwy. 40 and head west a couple of miles to Empire. About midway through Empire, turn left on Bard Creek Road. Park at the ball field on the edge of town. Pedal out of town on Bard Creek Road. For us this was a Sunday ride. Once clear of Empire there was no traffic. Maybe the Broncos-Seahawks game had something to do with it, but I suspect even on a normal day traffic is light.

The road is a flat, all-weather gravel road, for now. At 0.5 miles begin a moderate 10 percent climb. There is a variety of trees: aspen, lodgepole pine, Douglas fir, cottonwood, spruce, and ponderosa pine.

*West of Empire on Bard Creek Road*

In September the wildflowers had seen their day; expect to see a bunch on a midsummer ride. At less than 1.0 miles there is a short, tough, but makable 35-40 percent climb with a Georgetown view at the top. Look for bighorn sheep on the cliffs below, and grouse along the road.

After a short easy section, the road becomes skinnier and rougher as you climb higher and higher. Notice how lodgepole pines have taken over and become the predominant tree.

At 1.8 miles there is a four-wheel-drive road to the left; stay on the obvious main road for now and pedal through a grand stand of aspens — in fall it's all crunch, color, and smell. There is a campsite at 1.9 miles. There is a steep, 30-40 percent climb at 2.1 miles, a creek crossing at 2.2 miles, and another steep climb at 2.3 miles — all just practice for ... "Deadman's Hill" at 2.6 miles. I don't know where the name came from. I can guess. Actually it's not as bad as the name implies. It is, however, a steep, 35 percent-plus climb on loose gravel and rocks up to the 3.0 mile point.

After a respite at 3.0 miles, continue the climb at 3.1 miles. At 3.2 miles there is a road to the left that goes back to a campsite and an old beaver pond. This is a pretty nifty place to have lunch.

The Bard Creek Mine is at 3.8 miles. Climb on by and up to a Road Closed sign, straight ahead, at 4.1 miles. You can continue on the closed road — it is open to mountain bikers. It goes past an old sawmill and continues along Bard Creek for a couple of miles or so. For this ride, however, curl around to the right, drop a short distance, and then climb to an abandoned mine shaft at 4.2 miles. This is the end. The view is great. Be very careful on the return.

# West Chicago Creek Road

## 14

*Ride rating*
**Moderate**

*Skill level*
**Intermediate**

*Round trip*
**7.0 miles**

*Approximate ride time*
**1.3 hours**

*Starting elevation*
**8800 feet**

*Highest point*
**9800 feet**

*Maps*
**Arapaho National Forest**
**USGS 7.5-minute Idaho Springs, Georgetown**
**USGS 1:50 000-scale Clear Creek County**
**Trails Illustrated #104 Loveland Pass**

West Chicago Creek is easy to get to. There is a National Forest campground there, and some good hiking trails. It is a fairly busy road, but it's still a nice mountain bike route. For the most part, it is an easy and beginning ride. There is a strenuous and more advanced section that you can avoid.

Take I-70 to Idaho Springs and Colorado Hwy. 103, exit 240. Head southwest toward Mt. Evans. In less than 7 miles there is a West Chicago Creek Campground sign. This is West Chicago Creek Road.

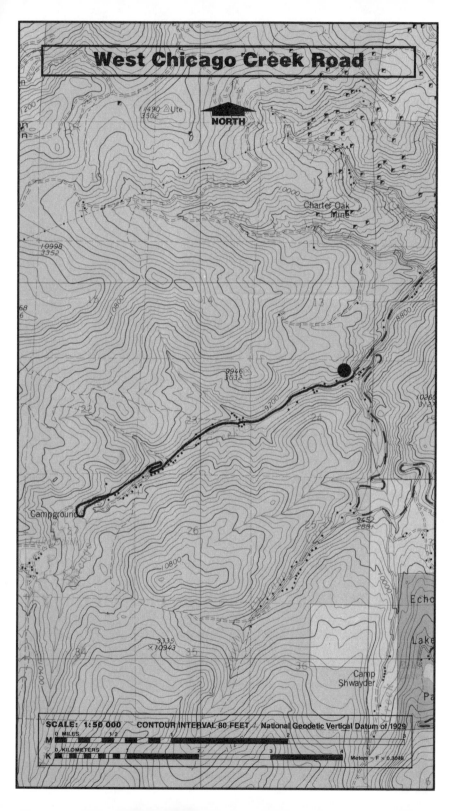

# West Chicago Creek Road

NORTH

Charter Oak Mine

Campground

Echo

Lake

Camp Shwayder

SCALE: 1:50 000   CONTOUR INTERVAL 80 FEET   National Geodetic Vertical Datum of 1929

This is the place. Park in the large parking area on the right side of the road and start pedaling up West Chicago Creek Road.

This is a wide, all-weather gravel road. It starts out as an easy incline. This was a weekend, fall ride, and the aspen were spectacular. Even with just about all of Denver hitting the hills to see the color, the traffic was not objectionable. A variety of trees, including Douglas fir, spruce, and lodgepole, share the area.

Pedal past the Arapaho National Forest sign in less than 0.5 miles. There is a residential area around 1.0 miles, followed by a meadow. This is a real pretty area with its aspen stands, meadow, and high mountains. At 2.0 miles the road is still good, but it's now a bit steeper at 10-15 percent. Because the road is in such good shape, consider this climb a piece of cake.

The West Chicago Creek Campground is at 2.9 miles. The Lake Edith trailhead parking lot is straight ahead; this is a popular hiking area. We, however, are

*West Chicago Creek Road*

*West Chicago Creek area*

going to take the road to the right, right by the campground entrance, and pedal up a 20-30 percent incline on an okay, single-lane, four-wheel-drive road. This is where the easy ride gets strenuous. Loose gravel compounds the task, but you really don't have to go very far. There is a campsite at 3.2 miles. At 3.3 miles take the road to the left. If you miss it, you'll hit a dead end in less than a mile. Now it's all down. The road starts out as a two-pather. After a short distance you will ride into a camping area. The road becomes a little obscure here. Bear to the left and continue down a moderate decline. There is a fork at 3.6 miles; go to the right. The road has become a wide path. It's very rocky, but also very short. Be careful. Intersect the regular road again at 3.9 miles. Make a left and cross under the gate by the trailhead lot. Pedal past the campground, past the road that took you to where you are now, and head back down to the start.

# Devils Canyon Loop

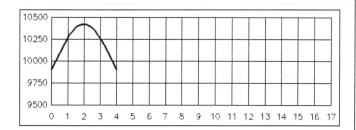

*Ride rating*
**Moderate/Strenuous**

*Skill level*
**Intermediate/Advanced**

*Round trip*
**4.0 miles**

*Approximate ride time*
**1.5 hours**

*Starting elevation*
**9900 feet**

*Highest point*
**10,400 feet**

*Maps*
**Arapaho National Forest**
**USGS 7.5-minute Idaho Springs**
**USGS 1:50 000-scale Clear Creek County**
**Trails Illustrated #104 Loveland Pass**

This is one of those places where you can ride all day or just pedal around for a couple of hours. Devils Canyon is a maze of roads. It is difficult to write a single concise route description. Don't hesitate to simply ride around. The area is fairly open — you can see where you have been and where you are going. However, consider taking a map and compass; while I don't think you will get lost and die, you could be late for supper. You can pedal all the way to Idaho Springs from here, but I'm not even going to try to tell you how.

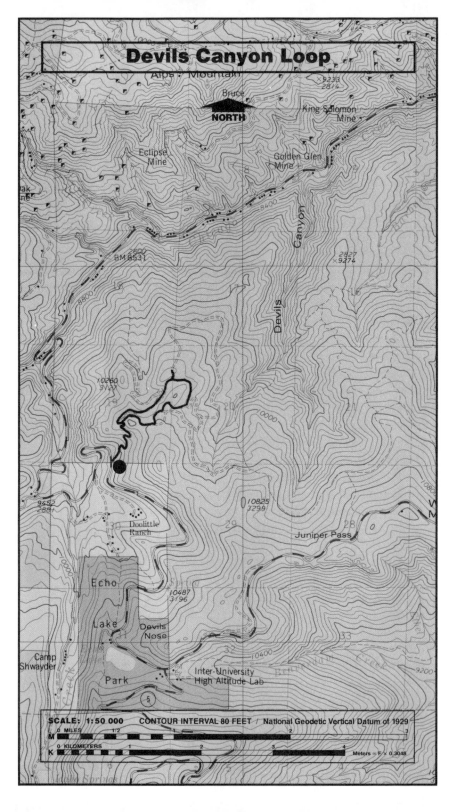

# Devils Canyon Loop

Alps Mountain

Bruce

**NORTH**

King Solomon
Mine

Eclipse
Mine

Golden Glen
Mine

×9233
2814

Oak
ine

8400

Devils

Canyon

2800
BM 8531

2827
9274

8800

116

×10260
3127

20

0000

9452
2881

◊10825
3299

29

Doolittle
Ranch

Juniper Pass

28

0

1080

W
M

Echo

10487
3196

Lake

Devils
Nose

33

Camp
Shwayder

Park

Inter-University
High Altitude Lab

32

10400

9200

5

**SCALE: 1:50 000**   CONTOUR INTERVAL 80 FEET / National Geodetic Vertical Datum of 1929

M   0 MILES        1/2              1                    2                    3

K   0 KILOMETERS        1              2              3              4        Meters = F × 0.3048

From Denver take I-70 to the Colorado Hwy. 74 El Rancho exit and head toward Evergreen. From Bergen Park take Colorado Hwy. 103 toward Mt. Evans and Echo Lake. Just Beyond Echo Lake watch for the Devils Canyon sign; it's on the right. Park on the wide shoulder on the right side of the road. Unload your bike and start climbing up Forest Route 246.

*Devils Canyon Loop*

This is a strenuous start up a 20-25 percent grade. Since you will be stopping along the way, be sure to look behind you — the Mt. Evans view is spectacular. I did this route on September 19. The aspens were yellow and Mt. Evans was white.

The first fork in the road is before 0.8 miles; head right. There is a campsite at 1.0 miles, and another at 1.2 miles. There is a fork in the road at this point; go left and down a rocky decline. Stay on the main road as you pass a side road at less than 1.3 miles. Turn right at 1.3 miles and left at 1.4 miles. Yes, this is a maze.

*Aspen in Devils Canyon*

There are a couple of mini-peaks to the left. You are an able rider if you can pedal the 50 yards up to the campsite located in the saddle between the little peaks. If you decide not to try, at least walk up for the view. Coming back down, make a hard left at the bottom of the hill. At 1.7 miles you are back on a more visible two-path road. Head left at 1.8 miles and climb a moderate grade up to another road junction at 2.1 miles. It's time for another diversion, so turn to the right and climb up to another good lookout at 2.2 miles. Turn around and head back to the last turn; this time turn right and start down a series of easy ups and downs. There is a Devils Canyon Tree Plantation sign at 2.8 miles. An old fellow in an old Bronco told me that in the '50s there was a "hell-of-a-fire back here." In the spring of 1983 the Forest Service planted fifty acres of lodgepole pines here.

At 3.1 miles climb through a nice stand of fat aspens, and then cruise down to the intersection at 3.2 miles. Head right and continue down to the end.

# Barbour Fork Loop

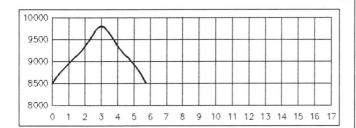

## 16

*Ride rating*
**Strenuous**

*Skill level*
**Intermediate/Advanced**

*Round trip*
**5.8 miles**

*Approximate ride time*
**2.0 hours**

*Starting elevation*
**8500 feet**

*Highest point*
**9800 feet**

*Maps*
**Arapaho National Forest**
**USGS 7.5-minute Idaho Springs**
**USGS 1:50 000-scale Clear Creek County**
**Trails Illustrated #104 Loveland Pass**

From outside of Idaho Springs, this route heads up toward Juniper Pass. The area between I-70, south of Idaho Springs, and Colorado Hwy. 103, Squaw Pass Road, is full of places to ride your mountain bike. I'd rate most of the area routes moderate to strenuous. You can ride for an hour or two. Or you can ride for a day or two. And you are only forty-five minutes from Denver. I like this route. I've done it a couple of times. It's not crowded — I have only seen six horses, one beat-up Scout, and a shiny new Isuzu along the way.

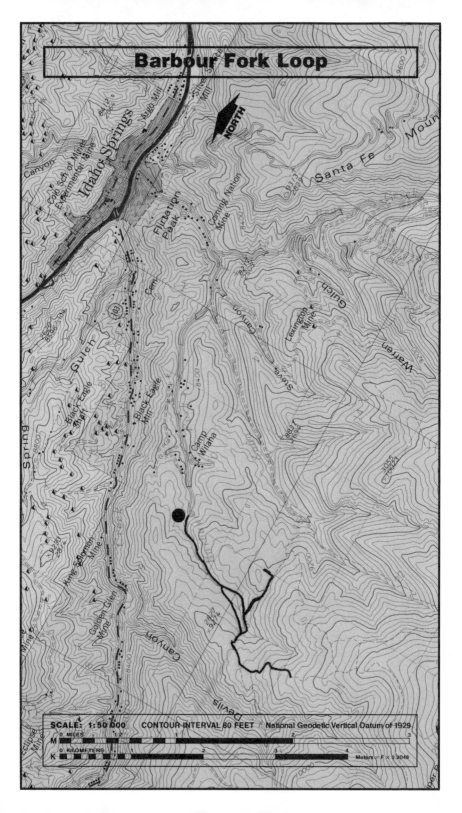

# Barbour Fork Loop

NORTH

SCALE: 1:50 000    CONTOUR INTERVAL 80 FEET    National Geodetic Vertical Datum of 1929

Once called Sacramento City, then Idaho City, then just plain Idaho, then Idahoe, Idaho Springs started out as a gold camp in 1860. Back in those days the canyon housed about five times the number of people there now. Idaho Springs was bigger than Denver. Look at the mountains — the mining scars remain.

From Denver take I-70 to the first Idaho Springs exit. Follow the Cental Business District signs along Miner Street to Soda Creek Road. Turn left, cross under I-70, pass the Indian Creek Springs Resort and continue for about 2 miles on Soda Creek Road to the local landfill. Continue on the obvious main, now gravel, road past the Clear Creek School District Camp to the large parking area less than 4 miles from Idaho Springs. Park and pedal past the gate and up Forest Route 194 — the four-wheel-drive road at the entrance to the parking lot. You can add 7 to 8 miles to the ride if you start in Idaho Springs.

The forest is a blend of ponderosa pine, aspen, cedar, Douglas fir, and spruce. The road is in pretty good shape. There are some short, steep, 30-35 percent inclines mixed in with a not-less-than-most-of-

The Barbour Fork loop

the-time-constant 10-15 percent incline. I think you get the message.

Note how the trees are changing as you climb into the next ecosystem. There is a road to the right at 0.7 miles; this is where you will come out later. For now continue straight ahead on this now quite rocky road. Bend to the right at 1.0 miles and ride through a nice open area. Bend to the left at 1.2 miles, continue up a 10-15 percent incline and through a tunnel of trees. The grade increases to 30 percent or so as you approach a fork in the road at 1.6 miles. Turn to the left and pedal up to the end of the road at 1.8 miles. The road becomes a single-path trail at this point; this is a good place to turn around and head in another direction. There is a private ranch in the area; stay on your side of the fence. There are some nice rock outcroppings to sit on while you enjoy the view.

Heading back down the way you came, go straight and cross the creek at 2.3 miles. This is the inter-section where, when coming up, you turned left. To go back the way you came, turn right. To continue this adventure, go straight, cross the creek, and ride up to a trashed-out campsite. Make a hard left and head west, and you guessed it, up. There is a closed road to the left at 2.4 miles; you can try it out later. For now continue on the main road, bend to the right, and climb another 30-35 percent incline.

There is an intersection with a couple of obscure roads at 2.6 miles; stay on the obvious main road and pedal into an open area at 2.7 miles. Bend to the right and climb up to another opening, and an old cabin site, at 2.8 miles. Continue straight up the hill and turn to the left at 3.2 miles. Pedal over a few easy ups and downs to the end at 3.5 miles. To the left, a single-path trail cuts past the remains of an old cabin. It's really kind of neat in here. There is a little creek. It's dark. On this day there was snow. This is a good place to sit and think. Why do you suppose someone built this cabin in such a cold place? If you own a pair of skins, I'll bet this is a good place to ski into.

Head back the way you came. When you get to the aforementioned trashed-out campsite, go straight and head down the open area on the left side of the creek. The road is a two-pather. It is fast. There are some soft spots — be careful. Intersect Forest Route 194 at 5.1 miles. Turn left and head back to the parking lot.

Barbour Fork
Loop

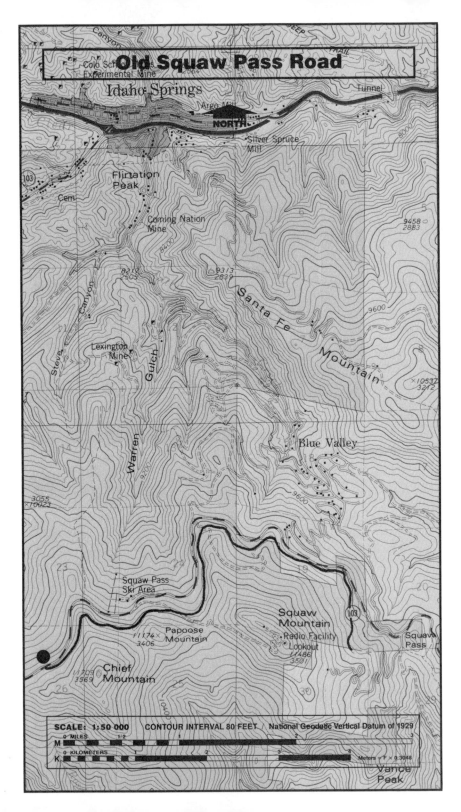

# Old Squaw Pass Road

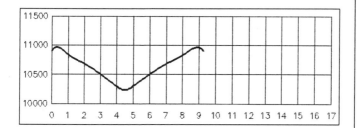

*Ride rating*
**Moderate/Strenuous**
*Skill level*
**Intermediate**
*Round trip*
**9.2 miles**
*Approximate ride time*
**2.5 hours**
*Starting elevation*
**10,900 feet**
*Highest point*
**11,000 feet**
*Maps*
**Arapaho National Forest**
**USGS 7.5-minute Idaho Springs, Squaw Pass**
**USGS 1:50 000-scale Clear Creek County**
**Trails Illustrated #104 Loveland Pass**

On this ride you can have an easy downhill cruise if you shuttle a car, or you can get your exercise by going down and then back up. This is a good ride for just about any rider — it's as strenuous as you want to make it. The Front Range views are spectacular, and part of the road is closed to motorized vehicles. Old Squaw Pass Road is also a good cross-country skiing route.

Old Squaw Pass Road parallels Colorado Hwy. 103 (the new Squaw Pass Road). While you will not need it, the Clear Creek County map is the only one listed above that shows the entire route on a single map. From Denver, take I-70 to the Colorado Hwy. 74 El Rancho exit and head toward Evergreen. From Bergen Park, take Colorado Hwy. 103 toward Mt. Evans and Echo Lake. Pass the old Squaw Pass ski area at around the 19-mile road marker and park in the large pull-off area, on the right, another mile down the road. You can't miss it. Chief Mountain (11,709 feet) looms to the east on the other side of the road. Walk your bike across the road, toward the mountain, up the bank, and onto the somewhat overgrown start of the old road. This is the place.

Ride around the new trees sprouting up on the old road and pedal up a short, easy incline. The new growth soon fades as you continue on this nonstop downhill run. The Front Range, Indian Peaks, and Continental Divide views to the northwest are spectacular. The road is in good shape. This route parallels Hwy. 103, so there is some road noise. This is the subalpine life zone; it is an Engelmann spruce-subalpine fir forest ecosystem.

At 1.6 miles the road kind of ends at a cliff. A new road crosses and cuts through the old one you are on. Ride (I was showing off) or walk your bike over the cliff (actually it's not that bad), cross the road, and continue down the same road you were on. There is a sign at this point announcing that the road is being considered for closure to motorized vehicles. Write the Forest Service and tell them that you think it's a good idea.

There is a side road to the right at 1.7 miles; continue on the main road. The road is still in good shape and it's fast. Be careful. Remember that there still might be a truck or two on this old road.

There is a campsite at 2.6 miles. At 2.7 miles the road becomes quite rocky. The decline is 15-20 percent — fun now, but wait for the return. Note how the lodgepoles have become the predominant tree as you lose elevation. At 3.1 miles there is a side road to the left that heads down to Hwy. 103. Don't turn yet; continue going straight and pass an old National Forest picnic area at 3.4 miles. From here the road is narrow and rocky. At 4.0 miles there is another side road to the left; remember this place. If you shuttled a car or are catching a ride, you can take this road back down to Hwy. 103. However, back on the high road, continue down a 20 percent grade, through a grand stand of fat aspens, and up to the road's end at 4.6 miles. Downtown Denver is straight ahead. The brown cloud extends as far along the Front Range as you can see. Well, there you have it — in less than one hour, a good look at nature's best and Denver's worst. Everything has been said. I think I'll just stay in the mountains and be smug.

*Old Squaw Pass Road*

Back on the road again, the return ride is strenuous, yet certainly makable by anyone who keeps it in low and takes a few breathers along the way. Plan on an hour or more to get back up — if you don't stop. Double your time if you do.

*Old Squaw Pass Road*

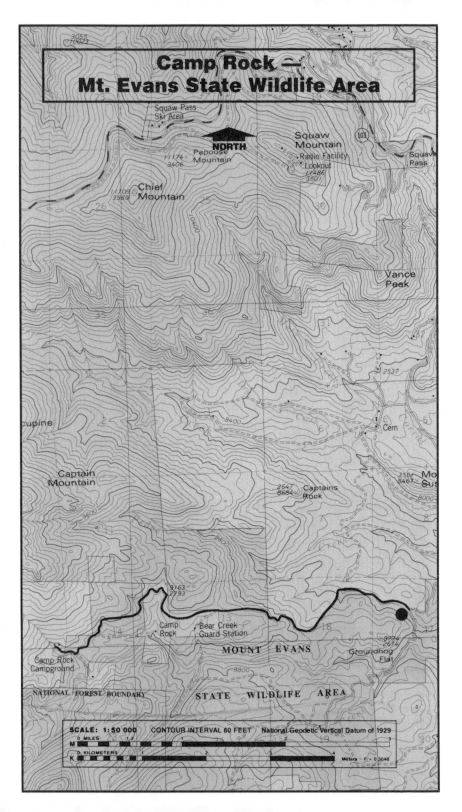

# Camp Rock —
# Mt. Evans State Wildlife Area

SCALE: 1:50 000    CONTOUR INTERVAL 80 FEET    National Geodetic Vertical Datum of 1929

# Camp Rock —
# Mt. Evans State Wildlife Area

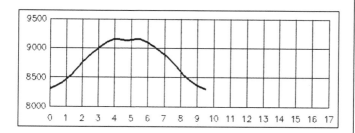

*Ride rating*
> **Moderate/Strenuous**

*Skill level*
> **Intermediate**

*Round trip*
> **9.6 miles**

*Approximate ride time*
> **2.25 hours**

*Starting elevation*
> **8300 feet**

*Highest point*
> **9200 feet**

*Maps*
> **Arapaho National Forest**
> **USGS 7.5-minute Harris Park, Meridian Hill**
> **USGS 1:50 000-scale Clear Creek County**
> **Trails Illustrated #104 Loveland Pass**

Camp Rock is located within the State Wildlife Area and it is a jumping-off point for the Mt. Evans Wilderness Area. It is closed from January 1 to June 15. It is a good, close-in, Evergreen-area ride. The road is in okay shape; if it were not, I would have rated this ride as strenuous — there are some arduous climbs. But don't let that scare you away; this is a nice place to visit. If you get tired, there's nothing wrong with walking now and then.

The Mt. Evans Wildlife Area is also known as the Elk Management Area. By 1900 hunters had killed

just about every elk in the Front Range. In 1913, 23
elk were brought here from Yellowstone National Park.
Today there are over 1000.

Evergreen was first called The Post, after Amos
Post, son-in-law of Thomas Bergen, the first settler,
who arrived back in 1859. Naturalist Charles
Christopher Parry discovered and named the Colorado
blue spruce right here in little old Evergreen. Parry is
also the fellow who named Grays and Torreys, a
couple of fourteeners, after two of his teachers. Spend
some time in Evergreen.

From downtown Evergreen, take Colorado Hwy.
74 to Upper Bear Creek Road. Upper Bear Creek Road
joins Hwy. 74 at the north end of Evergreen Lake.
Take Upper Bear Creek Road for about 6 miles, turn
right at the fork, drive past the sawmill, and continue
for another 2 miles to the next intersection. Cross
over the cattle guard and follow the signs to the State
Wildlife Area. Park in the large public parking area by
the picnic ground and start pedaling up to Camp Rock
on the road to the right as you enter the parking area.

There is some traffic on this road, but on this
Sunday afternoon it was not bad. There is a series of
easy ups and downs as you pass aspen, Douglas fir,
ponderosa pine, lodgepole, and spruce. At 0.5 miles
the forest opens, and there are some nice views just
as you head down a short, moderate, 20-30 percent
decline and back up a similar, but longer, incline.

In general the real climbing starts at around 1.0
miles. There are roses all along the road. There is a
nice viewpoint at 1.9 miles followed by a series of
ups and downs. The road is a bit rougher, but it's
still in pretty good shape. The Bear Creek Guard
Station is at 2.6 miles. The Lost Creek and Captain
Mountain trailheads, which go into the Mt. Evans
Wilderness Area, start at this point. Stay on the road
and take the roller coaster down to Camp Rock
Campground, the end, at 4.8 miles. This campground
is complete with a brick outhouse. You can hike into

the wilderness from this point.

This really is a good ride. Wildflowers abound. The mountains are grand. And you can get a pretty good workout — especially when you return up the hill you just came down.

*Camp Rock —*
*Mt. Evans State*
*Wildlife Area*

*Elk Management Area*

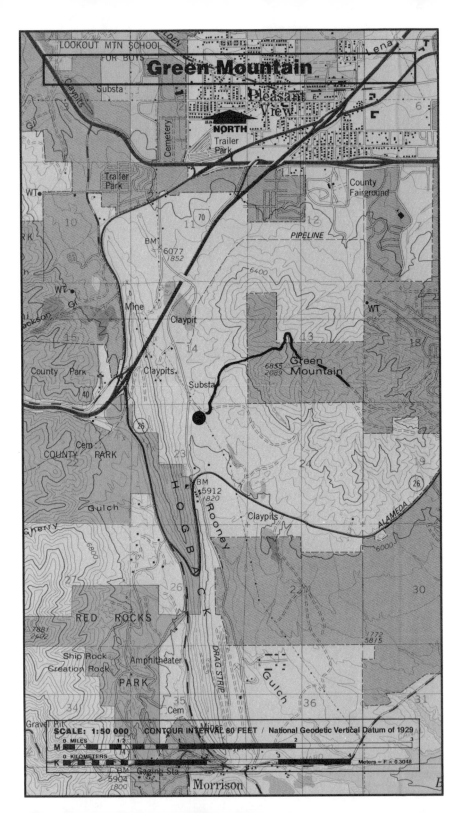

# Green Mountain

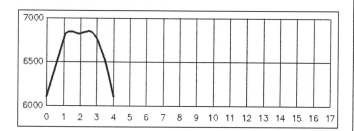

*Ride rating*
**Strenuous**
*Skill level*
**Advanced**
*Round trip*
**4.0 miles**
*Approximate ride time*
**1.5 hours**
*Starting elevation*
**6100 feet**
*Highest point*
**6800 feet**
*Maps*
**USGS 7.5-minute Morrison**
**USGS 1:50 000-scale Jefferson County - 1**

Depending on the snow conditions, you could probably ride on Green Mountain year-round. Getting to the top is hard — hence the rating. Once you're up it's a breeze. If you're not up to it, push your bike the mile or so to get to the top. This is an interesting, close-in ride. Green Mountain is laced together with roads and two-path trails; you can pedal from lunch to dinner. On a clear day the Front Range vista is wonderful. Even the view to the east is kind of interesting; it's like sitting on top of the watertower back home when I was a kid.

I rode this one after a heavy rain; the road to the top was in bad shape. Given some road improvements, the trip up could be handled by a beginner willing to work.

Green Mountain is north of Morrison, south of I-70, and on the west side of Lakewood. Hayden Green Mountain Park is administered by the City of Lakewood. This ride is in the park.

Frankly, a map is useless unless you want to identify landmarks; e.g., the great metropolis to the east with its majestic skyscrapers rising above the umber cloud. I haven't found a map that accurately depicts these trails; I'm not even sure if I have it perfect here. But don't worry, you can't get lost.

You can get there by taking Colorado Hwy. 74 through Morrison to Rooney Road or by taking I-70 to Colorado Hwy. 26 to Rooney Road. You can also get to Rooney Road from U.S. Hwy. 285, and from Alameda Parkway. It's easy to get to. From Rooney Road, follow the Open Space sign and turn east on the road by the electrical substation. Park in the large lot and pedal up Green Mountain.

Well, it's not that easy. If you are human, you will walk your bike less than 100 yards up the steep, rutted road directly in front of you. Turn right at the top of the ridge and continue up a 20-30 percent grade. If this road has been recently graded, this section won't be too bad. If it is muddy or rutted, you can expect to test your skill, strength, and endurance.

At 0.5 miles there is a 50-yard respite followed by a more moderate 15-20 percent incline. There are no trees here. No, you are not above tree line — these are the foothills. During the early summer this area is covered with wildflowers, but this was a fall ride; we were content with yucca and rose hips.

The road meets the Green Mountain and the John Hayden trails. Lookout Mountain is over to the left, it has towers on top. The Flatirons over Boulder are to the north. Red Rocks is farther south. Keep an eye out for Pikes Peak. And the ridge that runs along the east side of the Front Range is the Dakota Hogback, which is made up of Mesozoic rock, tilted up and facing west, all resulting from the uplift of the Front Range. I'm sure you have seen the cross section where I-70 cuts the hogback. If not, take a look while you're up here.

You can take either trail — left for a semi-flat loop, or right. We're headed right for this description, so pedal up a moderate incline to a Denver overlook at 1.2 miles. The road improves as you finally start down an easy decline at 1.3 miles. It's real pleasant up here; I relaxed and let my mind wander, and I executed a complete flip over my handlebars. I've never done that before. It hurt. Be careful; there is some deep, loose gravel on the road.

Ridge Top Trail and Green Mountain Trail intersect at 1.5 miles. Continue to the right on Green Mountain Trail — do Ridge Top later. Take the roller coaster down to the communication tower at 2.0 miles. This is where I turned around and started back. I'll return for more.

*Atop Green Mountain*

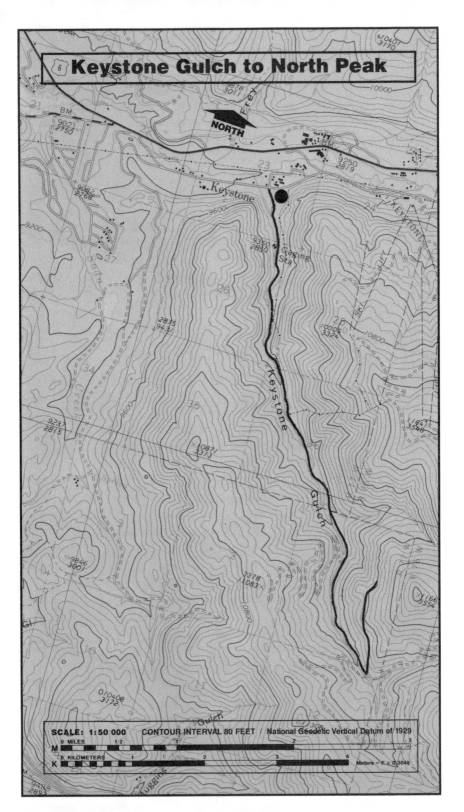

# 6 Keystone Gulch to North Peak

NORTH

SCALE: 1:50 000    CONTOUR INTERVAL 80 FEET    National Geodetic Vertical Datum of 1929

0 MILES    1/2    1    2    3

0 KILOMETERS    1    2    3    4    Meters = F. x 0.3048

# Keystone Gulch to North Peak

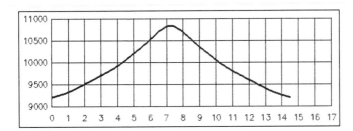

*Ride rating*
**Moderate/Strenuous**

*Skill level*
**Intermediate**

*Round trip*
**14.4 miles**

*Approximate ride time*
**3.0 hours**

*Starting elevation*
**9200 feet**

*Highest point*
**10,800 feet**

*Maps*
**Arapaho National Forest**
**USGS 7.5-minute Keystone**
**USGS 1:50 000-scale Summit County - 2**
**Trails Illustrated #104 Loveland Pass**

This is a good ride. It can be quite a workout for a strong and experienced rider and a challenge for a beginner. The late-summer spectacle of a snowcapped Continental Divide is a harbinger of things to come. This is Keystone, big-time ski country. Soon a swarm of skiers will be buzzing around this mountain. Today things are a little slower.

Keystone Creek runs down the gulch and into the Snake River. Tim Kelley says that the creek is fair for small brookies, but that the Snake is not so hot. A hundred years ago the bright lights were up the valley in Montezuma. Today the mines are quiet, the town is sleepy, history remains. Aladdin's Lamp, Brittle Silver, Equity, Hunkidori, Lucky Baldwin, Silver Wave, Star of the West, and Winning Card are the names that tell us about the dreams of miners. Today the gold is white and the silver is green — and it's located in Keystone.

Keystone is between Dillon and Loveland Pass. Dillon is named after a prospector who got lost in the area. You can row your boat over the original town — it is entirely under the water of Dillon Reservoir. Take I-70 to U.S. Hwy. 6, east of the Eisenhower Tunnel, and approach Keystone from the east, or take I-70 to U.S. Hwy. 6 at Dillon/Silverthorne and approach Keystone from the west. Follow the signs and park in the skier's parking lot on the east side of the ski area, just off of U.S. Hwy. 6 and Montezuma Road. Pedal into the ski village and head east on Soda Ridge Road to Keystone Gulch. Turn left and south and head up the gulch along Keystone Creek. You could have driven to this point and parked on the right side of the road, but that wouldn't have been as much fun.

As you might expect, you start pedaling up a moderate incline on a pretty good unimproved road. There are a few campsites along the route; the first one is at around 1.0 miles. At 1.7 miles the grade increases to 10-15 percent and levels off for a while at 2.1 miles. On this day there were more horses than cars. In fact, at this point we saw more bears than cars. That's right. Actually it was one bear. I only saw its hind end scooting up and over the hill, but it was a bear — a honey brown colored black bear. It's not every day that I get to tell you about a bear; it sure beats yakking about lodgepole pine. Ursus americanus can grow to five feet in length and weigh up to 400 pounds. Black bears range in color from blond to black. They are omnivorous; they seldom pass up anything from grass, seeds, nuts, and eggs, to fish, gophers, and garbage. I suspect that a black bear can

shinny up a tree faster than you. Black bears are generally not dangerous to man. The reverse, of course, is
not true.

Back on the road, the North Peak ski lifts come
into view at 3.2 miles. You will probably also notice
that the incline is up a bit and the road is getting
rougher. Bend to the right by the lifts and continue
up a 15-20 percent incline as the lodgepole pine and
aspen give way to spruce and fir. There is an explorable four-wheel-drive road to the right at 3.6 miles;
for now stay on the obvious main road and continue
up. The grade increases to 20 percent at 5.0 miles
and to 30 percent at 5.8 miles. The climb seems
interminable. It's getting hard. I'm getting tired. but
Terry, my riding partner, is younger, and ... I'll rest
when it looks like he's going to stop — if you know
what I mean.

After 6.0 miles the Divide comes into view. Mt.
Guyot (13,370 feet) is to the south. There is a gate at
6.6 miles. The Erickson Mine is to the right. This
mine produced ore from the 1880s till the 1930s. The
mine extends 250 feet down and another 250 feet
into Keystone Mountain. We're headed to the top of

*Keystone Gulch
to North Peak*

*Keystone on the way to North Peak*

North Peak, so go through the gate, past the No Motorized Vehicles sign, and continue up the road to the top.

There are some 40 percent inclines along the way. Don't be afraid to walk. The end is at 7.2 miles. There is a picnic table at the top. Dillon Reservoir is to the west. Breckenridge is to the south. Take it easy on the return — it's rocky and fast. I say that a lot, don't I?

# Montezuma Area — Webster Pass

21

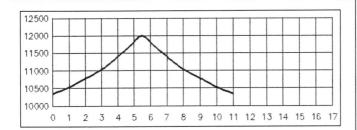

*Ride rating*
**Strenuous**
*Skill level*
**Intermediate**
*Round trip*
**11.0 miles**
*Approximate ride time*
**3.0 hours**
*Starting elevation*
**10,350 feet**
*Highest point*
**12,096 feet**
*Maps*
**Arapaho National Forest**
**USGS 7.5-minute Montezuma**
**USGS 1:50 000-scale Summit County - 2**
**Trails Illustrated #104 Loveland Pass**

There is a cluster of mountain biking routes in the Montezuma area. Montezuma is about 5 miles east of Keystone. This area is also popular with the motorized crowd; so start early or ride when the Broncos are playing. Other well-known Montezuma area routes are Peru Creek, Saints John Creek, Radical Hill, and Deer Creek. I suspect you'll discover more if you ask a local.

The Webster Pass route takes you above timber line and to the Continental Divide. This was once a toll route to the Montezuma area mines. Montezuma

117

# Montezuma Area — Webster Pass

USLM Adrian

Chihuahua

USLM
BM 3176
×10421

**NORTH**

Brittle Silver
Mountain ×12228
3727

BM
10004
3049

Tiptop
Peak ×12053
3674

Morgan
Peak

Collier

Silver
Mountain

Cem
Montezuma

Gulch

Morgan

Mountain

CONTINENTAL

Sill
Mine

Britannic
Mine

Bullion
Mine

4017
13180

4017
13180

Bell
Mine

BM
10567
3221

Sullivan
Mountain

Sullivan
Mtn

×2441
3792

•3959
BM 11019

Geneva
Peak

Mohawk
Mine

Geneva
Peak

11804
3598

×12602
3841

×12367
3769

Teller Mountain

DIVIDE

Whale
Mine

BM
1209

Webster
Pass

Red
Cone

Handcart

**SCALE: 1:50 000** **CONTOUR INTERVAL 80 FEET** National Geodetic Vertical Datum of 1929

0 MILES 1/2 1 1 1/2 2 5/8 3
**M**

0 KILOMETERS 1 2 3 4
**K** Meters = F × 0.3048

Missouri
Mine USLM

is the site of the first Colorado silver find. Founded in 1865, it boasted over 700 people by 1890. Montezuma not only survived the silver rush, but also survived five major fires.

Take U.S. Hwy. 6 to Keystone. Find Montezuma Road on the east end of Keystone and turn south. If you are coming from Loveland Pass that's a left. Almost immediately veer to the left, past a parking area for the ski hill, and continue 5 miles or so to the town of Montezuma.

Park in Montezuma and pedal south out of town, on Montezuma Road, 1 mile to Webster Pass Road. Montezuma Road is gentle and all-weather gravel. Turn left on Webster Pass Road; it's marked. And it's steep. But it's not that long.

Webster Pass Road is a rocky four-wheel-drive road. In general, expect to climb 10-20 percent grades the entire trip up Webster Pass.

After less than 2 miles you'll come to a National Forest sign board. Check these when you see them. On a July ride, Handcart Road and Radical Hill Road were both blocked by snow.

*Beaver pond along the way to Webster Pass*

After 2 miles there is a big beaver pond to the right. If you are taking a midsummer tour, you will be treated to columbines, yellow paintbrush, and more. As you might expect at this elevation, the predominant trees are subalpine fir and Engelmann spruce.

There is a nice open area with 360-degree views at about 2.5 miles. The Snake River flows over the road at this point. In July the water was knee-high and cold. If you pick your way through the shallow spots, you can ride it and almost stay dry. After the crossing you are confronted with a 20-30 percent incline as you approach timberline.

It's a pretty constant 20 percent climb at 3.5 miles. At 3.8 miles there is a fork in the road. To the right is Radical Hill and Deer Creek. To the left is Webster Pass. Go left and climb the final 1.75 miles to the pass. The road has a lot of switchbacks. It is steep. It has a lot of loose stones on it. The ride is arduous but worth every calorie.

Webster Pass is at 12,400 feet. There is a great South Park view. While looking at South Park, Red Cone is the red mountain to your left, and Handcart Peak is to your right. If you are lucky you'll see kings crown, alpine buttercup, alpine sunflower, alpine forget-me-not, alpine flock, showy daisy, and sky pilot.

If the road is not blocked by snow, you can take Handcart Road down off the pass and continue all the way to U.S. Hwy. 285. I have tried this ride from the other side, coming up from U.S. Hwy. 285; there seems to be more traffic from that direction. For this tour it's back the way we came.

# Kenosha Creek

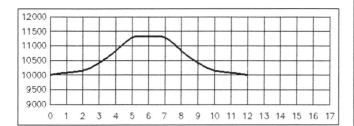

## 22

*Ride rating*
   **Moderate**
*Skill level*
   **Intermediate**
*Round trip*
   **12.2 miles**
*Approximate ride time*
   **3.5 hours**
*Starting elevation*
   **10,000 feet**
*Highest point*
   **11,400 feet**
*Maps*
   **Pike National Forest**
   **USGS 7.5-minute Mt. Logan, Jefferson**
   **USGS 1:50 000-scale Park County - 1, 2**


Memorial Day 1987. A muddy road, short pants and snow, short breath and bike seatitis; this was the first serious ride of a new season — it was wonderful. No matter what you think, five months of skiing will not prepare you for three hours of riding. But just getting into the mountains, just smelling that cold spring air, just feeling that hot sun and just ... well, I think you get the idea — this is fun.

From the campground at Kenosha Pass, this ride heads east, up Kenosha Creek and toward the Kenosha Mountains. Kenosha means pike (as in fish). Kenosha Creek flows into the North Fork of the South Platte.

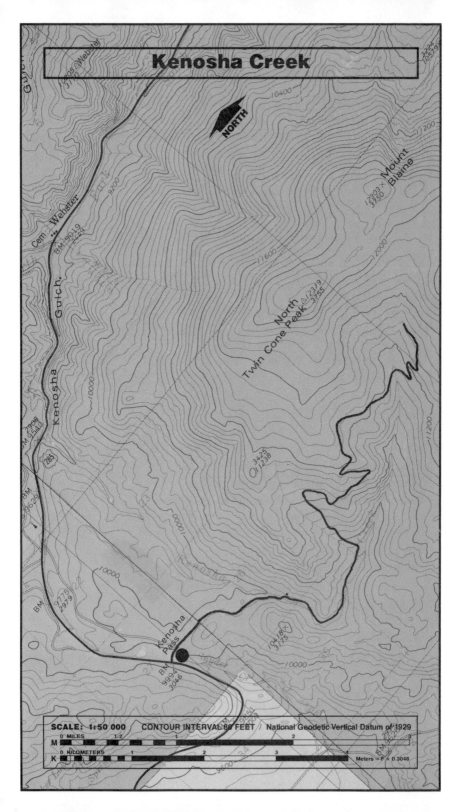

# Kenosha Creek

NORTH

SCALE: 1:50 000    CONTOUR INTERVAL 80 FEET    National Geodetic Vertical Datum of 1929

0 MILES    1/2    1    2    3

0 KILOMETERS    1    2    3    4    Meters > F × 0.3048

It is not considered a fishing hot spot. The pass, gulch, creek, and range were named by a stagecoach driver from Kenosha, Wisconsin. Now I don't know if you've ever been to Kenosha, but I can tell you from experience that Kenosha does not look like this. Probably for this reason, I have always poo-pooed the Kenosha Pass area — that was a mistake. There are some fine mountain biking routes along 285.

*Kenosha Creek*

If you are toting your own map, note that this ride covers two maps with the bulk of it on either the USGS 7.5-minute Mt. Logan or Park County-2. Park County-2 is more up-to-date.

The Kenosha Pass Pike (as in Lt. Zebulon) National Forest campground is located at Kenosha Pass, southwest of Denver between Bailey and Fairplay on U.S. Hwy. 285. From Denver turn left and park in the large parking area along 285. Pedal into the campground and then head right and up a 5-10 percent incline through the lodgepole and into the aspen and spruce on an okay dirt road. There are several primitive campsites along the route. I just left it in granny and experienced the day — at least for a while. This ride starts out easy but becomes moderately strenuous after 3 miles or so.

Stay on the obvious main road at 0.7 miles. At 0.8 miles the road becomes a series of ups and downs as you ride toward a grand aspen stand. There is a Forest Service gate at 1.0 miles — close it behind you. There are beaver ponds all along the creek.

Pass private property at 1.3 miles. On this date, the road was muddy — real muddy, like grease, but only for 100 yards or so. There is a little red house at 1.6 miles after which the road gets a bit rocky. We saw evidence (a euphemism) of elk, but no elk. At 1.7 miles, the beaver ponds and aspen stand, where the beavers were obviously busy, are interesting. Aspens are both construction material and food for these big rodents. A beaver can fell a five-inch aspen in three minutes. They are active year-round. They are nocturnal.

The snowcaps are in view at 1.7 miles, and I saw my first Bud Light can at 2.0 miles. At 2.0 miles there is a road to the left; stay on the main road and continue through the aspens. Note the heavily browsed and rubbed aspens. Elk eat aspen leaves, twigs, and bark. Aspen trunks are used by bull elk for scratching posts to rub the dry velvet from their antlers in late summer.

At 2.2 miles watch for the beaver lodge. At 2.3 miles you are still climbing, and at 2.3 miles there is a short, steep 30 percent incline. Pass through the gate at 2.6 miles and continue this prolonged climb. There are glimpses of snowcapped mountains along the way, and a South Park view at 4.4 miles. Large mountain valleys, meadows, and grasslands are called "parks," as in wild game park or preserve. The Colorado Rocky Mountains are separated by four large high-altitude valleys: North Park, South Park, Middle

*Kenosha Creek area*

Park, and the San Luis Valley. South Park covers roughly 900 square miles.

Just as you want to stop climbing, there is a flat spot followed by one last steep incline at 4.7 miles. The trees change from aspen and lodgepole to Engelmann spruce as you pass from the montane to subalpine life zone. The road flattens out and then becomes rocky as you head down and into a pretty meadow at 6.0 miles. The view really opens up along this last stretch. The main road ends in a fork at 6.1 miles. A rough four-wheel-drive road heads up in either direction. I plan to try these two later. Given good conditions, I wouldn't hesitate to drive a four-wheel-drive truck to this point. For now it's a fast trip back to the start.

*Kenosha Creek*

# Bill Tyler Gulch to Gibbs Gulch

NORTH

Shawnee Peak

Craig Gulch

RIVER

Par

Bill Tyler Gulch

Gibbs Gulch

Shawnee

Sna

Gulch

McArthur

Brookside

Gulch

Glenisle

Campground

SCALE: 1:50 000     CONTOUR INTERVAL 80 FEET     National Geodetic Vertical Datum of 1929

M   0 MILES   1 2                    1

K   0 KILOMETERS   1                    2                    3                    4        Meters = Ft × 0.3048

Corbin Gulch

Bailey

# Bill Tyler Gulch to Gibbs Gulch

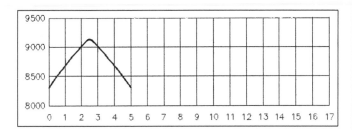

## 23

*Ride rating*
**Strenuous**
*Skill level*
**Intermediate**
*Round trip*
**5.0 miles**
*Approximate ride time*
**1.5 hours**
*Starting elevation*
**8300 feet**
*Highest point*
**9200 feet**
*Maps*
**Pike National Forest**
**USGS 7.5-minute Shawnee**
**USGS 1:50 000-scale Park County · 2**

This Shawnee area route runs up one gulch and over to another. The beginning is not as hard as the end. Shawnee is on U.S. Hwy. 285 between Bailey and Kenosha Pass. I like biking in this part of the Front Range. It's easy to get to. It's close to home, so short afternoon outings are within reason. And do you know what? It's not trashed-out like other close-in parts of our National Forest.

This was a Fourth of July weekend ride. We did not see even one other person on this route. The wildflowers were wild; we saw scarlet gilia, Indian paintbrush, Indian blanket, roses, vetch, shooting stars, mountain bluebells, columbine, and more.

I suspect that there are ghosts on 285. Placer gold was discovered around Breckenridge during the summer of 1859. Miners, merchants, and other fortune seekers needed a way to get to the gold. There was an old Ute trail — fine for ponies, but not so hot for wagons. So in 1867 a road was opened that started in Morrison, continued up Turkey Creek Canyon, passed through Bailey, climbed over Kenosha Pass, and dropped down into South Park. Sounds like present-day U.S. 285, doesn't it? Think about what it was like in 1867 as you drive to Shawnee. You're in a stage-coach. Maybe you're a New York newspaper reporter starting an assignment in Fairplay, or maybe you're a Chicago girl heading for a dance hall in Breckenridge. Or how about a minister, a mechant, the blacksmith's wife, the new sheriff, a lawyer? I wish I could really go back there for just one day.

From Denver take U.S. Hwy. 285 toward Fairplay. Shawnee is just after Platte Canyon High School. About 0.5 miles past Shawnee, pass the Department of Highways' gravel pit and shed and continue for a short distance to Forest Route 116; it's on the left side of the road. Park in the wide spot between the cattle guard and the highway.

Cross over the cattle guard and pedal up the rutted dirt road. The incline grade soon increases to 15-20 percent. There are some nice Platte River Mountain Range views to the south. There is a side road, closed to motorized vehicles, to the right at 0.7 miles. Give it a try if you have the time. For this description though, it's straight ahead on the main road and up a 20 percent incline.

Pedal through a grove of ponderosa pine, aspen, and Douglas fir. Cross the creek at 0.9 miles, continue past another side road to the right, and then cruise down a short hill and back up to a flat spot at 1.1 miles.

Start climbing again. Some spots get over 30

percent. This is pretty arduous; just when you think it should get easier, it gets harder. There is a fork in the road at 1.7 miles; go right and up — it's too early to think about going down. At 2.0 miles the trees are the same, but the incline grade is now up around 40 percent. I do my best on short, steep inclines when I use a mid-range gear and stand on the pedals. I do my best on long, steep inclines when I stay in low and sit.

There is a campsite at 2.2 miles. The ecosystem is slowly changing as you gain altitude; there's still a mixture of trees, but now there are fewer ponderosa pines and more spruce, lodgepole pine, and aspen — fat green aspen. It's still all up, and it's still steep from 2.3 miles to the end at 2.5 miles. The main road ends in a wide spot with a rough and steep single-path trail leading into the forest.

The return can be tricky. Depending on your skill level, you might consider walking some of the declines. The return views of the white mountain peaks are nice — just be sure you watch where you are going.

*Snow on the range south of Shawnee*

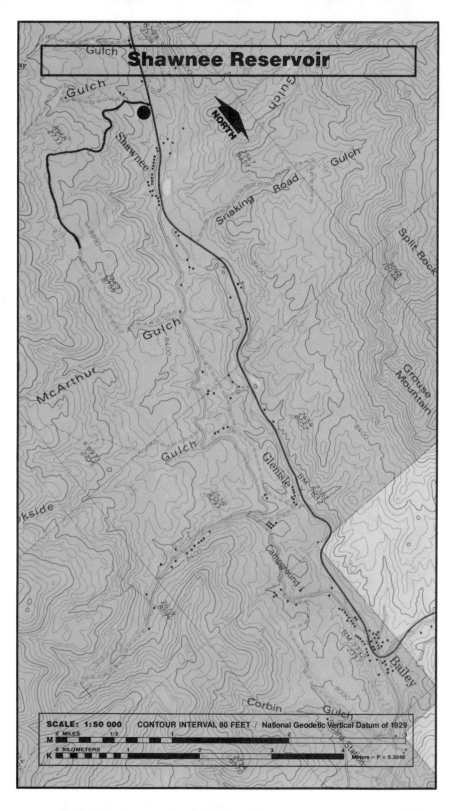

# Shawnee Reservoir

NORTH

SCALE: 1:50 000    CONTOUR INTERVAL 80 FEET / National Geodetic Vertical Datum of 1929

M   0 MILES        1/2              1                          2                          3

K   0 KILOMETERS        1              2              3              4        Meters = F × 0.3048

# Shawnee Reservoir

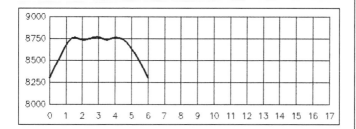

*Ride rating*
**Moderate/Strenuous**
*Skill level*
**Intermediate**
*Round trip*
**6.0 miles**
*Approximate ride time*
**1.5 hours**
*Starting elevation*
**8300 feet**
*Highest point*
**8800 feet**
*Maps*
**Pike National Forest**
**USGS 7.5-minute Shawnee**
**USGS 1:50 000-scale Park County - 2**

I just couldn't come up with a good name for this one; no one has named anything in the area. Maybe we should hang a name on one of the local mountains — something like "Bill's Peak." I like the sound of it; you know ... this ride starts west of Shawnee, heads south past the Shawnee water reservoir and ends on the south side of Bills Peak (8944 feet).

This is a nice ride. You can lengthen it by taking a side road here or there. There is camping in the area. Save your lunch for the end of the road; it's real pretty up there. On a Sunday afternoon in July, we saw only one vehicle on this road.

*Shawnee
Reservoir*

Shawnee is on U.S. Hwy. 285 between Bailey and Kenosha Pass. Back in 1880, folks from the Colorado & Southern Railway named it after Shawnee Peak (11,917 feet) in the Platte River Mountains to the south.

From Denver take U.S. Hwy. 285 toward Fairplay. Shawnee is just after Platte Canyon High School. About 0.5 miles past Shawnee, turn left at the Department of Highways' gravel pit and shed and park by the Pike National Forest access sign by the yellow cattle guard. You could have parked in Shawnee, but I wouldn't ask anyone to pedal on Hwy. 285. There is a No Trespassing sign — if you stay off the gravel piles and head for the forest, you'll be legal.

Make a hard left on the other side of the cattle guard and follow the sign into the National Forest on Forest Route 115, a two-path road at this point. Things get rough real quick. The road gets rocky and rutty, and the incline increases to about 20 percent. I think it gets worse up to 1.0 miles.

There is a mixture of trees; aspen, ponderosa pine, Douglas fir, and blue spruce. This was a July ride, and the wildflowers were out.

There is a fork in the road at 1.0 miles; head left and continue up this protracted climb to a gate at 1.2 miles. This is a good place to rest and take in the view. Soon the road levels off in a nice aspen grove. After a bit more climbing, there is a meadow at 1.5 miles followed by a fenced mini-reservoir at 1.8 miles. Stay awhile. Watch the swallows skim the surface. We saw snow in the mountains and elk tracks in the mud.

You can finally go down a hill at 1.9 miles. There is a side road to the right at 2.1 miles. Stay on the main road, and if it is summer, pedal through a field of iris, Indian paintbrush, columbine, false lupine, and probably a whole lot more. This meadow is flush with flowers, lots of flowers.

You start climbing again, and the road becomes a two-pather again at 2.3 miles. The rest of the route is a roller coaster of easy ups and downs. There is a little pond and then a road to the right at 2.7 miles. Check it out later; for now, keep left and continue to the end at 3.0 miles. The trees are lodgepole pines. There is a pond here. Shooting stars adorn the roadside.

*Shawnee Reservoir*

*South of Shawnee*

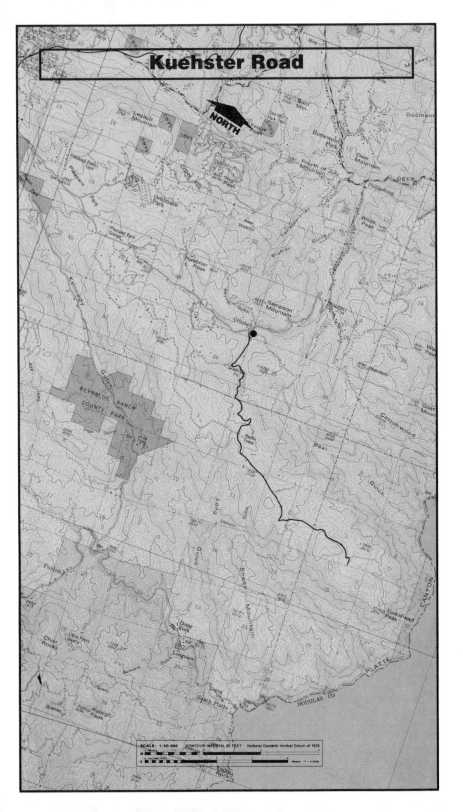

# Kuehster Road

NORTH

SCALE: 1:50 000    CONTOUR INTERVAL 80 FEET    National Geodetic Vertical Datum of 1929

# Kuehster Road

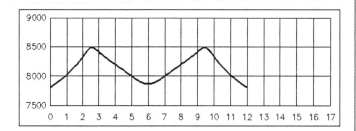

## 25

*Ride rating*
**Moderate**
*Skill level*
**Beginning**
*Round trip*
**12.0 miles**
*Approximate ride time*
**2.0 hours**
*Starting elevation*
**7800 feet**
*Highest point*
**8500 feet**
*Maps*
**Pike National Forest**
**USGS 7.5-minute Platte Canyon**
**USGS 1:50 000-scale Jefferson County - 2**
**Trails Illustrated #135 Rampart Range**

Yes, this is a surprise. Serendipity I guess. There are some really grand views along this route. Kuehster Road is an all-weather, county-maintained, gravel road southeast of Conifer. It's close to the metro area and it's easy to ride. Oh, there are some protracted climbs along the way, but I wouldn't call them strenuous — maybe moderately strenuous; so on balance this ride gets a moderate rating. This is a dead-end road; at quitting time, there was hardly any traffic. There are a few side roads along the route — extend your ride by exploring one or more of them.

*Kuehster Road*

From Denver, take U.S. Hwy. 285 south to the stoplight in Conifer. Turn left on Pleasant Park Road and drive about 6 miles or so to Critchel. Now Critchel isn't exactly Conifer, so don't miss it; consider taking a map so you don't. Kuehster Road is the main road on the right. You can park in the small lot on the right side after you turn onto Kuehster Road.

The ride starts with a steady, 10-15 percent climb up to a radio tower at 2.7 miles. From here it's pretty flat. There is a typical foothills variety of trees with aspen, spruce, ponderosa pine, and Douglas fir along the way. At about 3.0 miles there is a little red building to the right — Lamb School, an old Jefferson County schoolhouse.

To the right there are some fine vistas — the Wellington Lake area and the Castle. There is a series of easy ups and downs between 4.0 and 5.0 miles along with a Denver, Chatfield Lake, and plains view on one side and a Cripple Creek view on the other.

You're back in the trees at 5.2 miles. Watch for grouse. After crossing a cattle guard at 5.7 miles, start down a moderate decline past a hayfield on the left, and at 6.0 miles, ride around the big bend to the

*Old log houses on Kuehster Road*

point where the ranch at the end of the road comes into view. Scrub oak (Gambel oak) covers the hillside. There were even a few wildflowers in September. This is a good place to turn around — no sense bugging the folks at the end. You can build up some speed on the return. Watch for traffic.

*Kuehster Road*

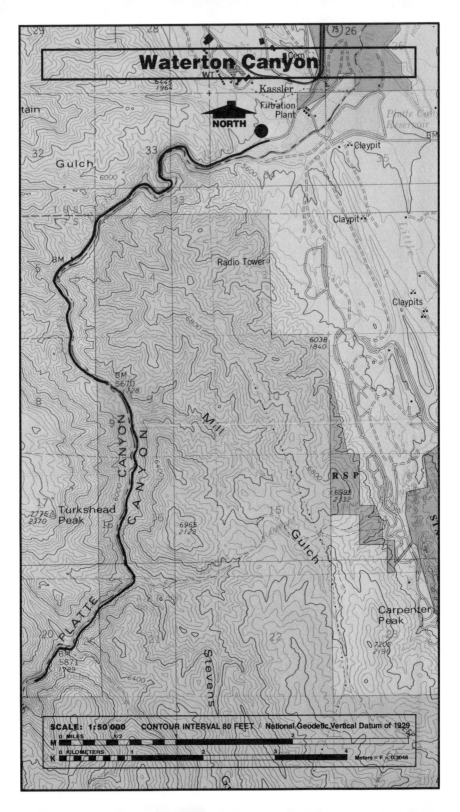

# Waterton Canyon

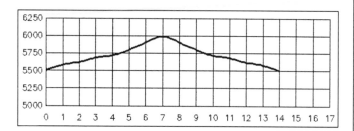

## 26

*Ride rating*
### Easy
*Skill level*
### Beginning
*Round trip*
### 14.0 miles
*Approximate ride time*
### 2.25 hours
*Starting elevation*
### 5600 feet
*Highest point*
### 6000 feet
*Maps*
### Pike National Forest
### USGS 7.5-minute Platte Canyon, Kassler
### USGS 1:50 000-scale Jefferson County - 2,
###    Douglas County - 1
### Trails Illustrated #135 Rampart Range

This is a fun ride. It's not a wilderness adventure. It's not hard to do. There are no cars. It's a nice outing. Since the road is covered with gravel, your friends can get away with their ten-speed racers. The road runs along the Platte River. This is a scenic, metro-area route; expect to see other bikers, hikers, and equestrians along the way. We saw a few stringers of trout, and, in September, even a few wildflowers.

From Denver, head south on Colorado Hwy. 75

past the Chatfield State Recreation Area, and just before the Martin Marietta complex, follow the Waterton Canyon Recreational Area sign to the left and then quickly turn to the right. Just up the road is a large parking lot. This is the place.

The Waterton Canyon Recreational Area is jointly administered by the Denver Water Board, the Forest Service, and the BLM. Motor vehicles are not allowed beyond the lot, so carry your bike through the special gate and head up the canyon. Oh, by the way, there are rattlesnakes in the area. We saw a large (three-foot) Prairie rattler on the road. A rattlesnake would rather slither than fight; but don't go and stick your hand behind a rock or tease a snake. They can strike out a third to a half of their length from any position. If you see one, respect it and consider yourself lucky to see one in the wild.

This road is wide and relatively flat. Oh, there are a few small ups and downs; but it's really pretty easy

*Waterton Canyon*

for the first few miles. The road surface is old pavement and gravel. At around 5.0 miles the road gets a tad steeper.

The Strontia Springs Dam is at 6.4 miles. It holds back Bear Creek. If you don't know it's there, this dam really takes you by surprise — it's big.

*Waterton Canyon*

After the dam, the road gets smaller, rougher, and steeper. There is an extended 5-10 percent climb up to the gate at 7.0 miles. The Colorado Trail joins the road at this point. The Colorado Trail, Trail #1776, is an old four-wheel-drive trail here. You can ride up, and I do mean up, the trail for a while, or head back.

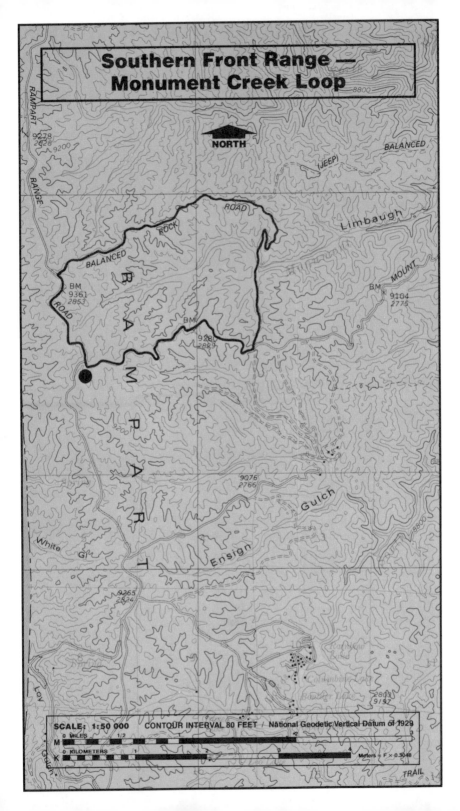

# Southern Front Range —
# Monument Creek Loop

**NORTH**

SCALE: 1:50 000    CONTOUR INTERVAL 80 FEET / National Geodetic Vertical Datum of 1929

# Southern Front Range — Monument Creek Loop

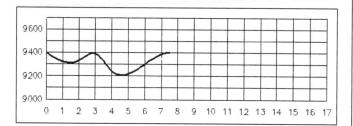

*Ride rating*

**Moderate**

*Skill level*

**Beginning**

*Round trip*

**7.5 miles**

*Approximate ride time*

**1.0 hours**

*Starting elevation*

**9400 feet**

*Highest point*

**9400 feet**

*Maps*

**Pike National Forest**

**USGS 7.5-minute Mount Deception, Palmer Lake**

**USGS 1:50 000-scale El Paso County - 1**

There are several routes between Buffalo Creek and Woodland Park. Rides such as the Wellington Lake Loop, the Buffalo Creek Loop, and Painted Rocks Campground to Westcreek are described in *Bicycling the Backcountry*. This is a high-use area — expect traffic. I have started other rides in this area only to turn around when the traffic and the people and the trash got to be too much. I know of some single-path hiking trails, but I am reluctant to start a Rampart Range hiker-biker controversy.

This ride, along with those mentioned above, are all on gravel roads. They are all pretty rides. Traffic

was not bad. This is a Rampart Range ride. This area,
north of Woodland Park, is popular with motorcycle
and ATV riders, but this particular tour is on roads
that are apparently not as popular with these folks.
On an after-supper tour I didn't see a single motorized
vehicle.

The reason for the Monument Creek moniker is
obvious. Vertical monuments, red monoliths, mark the
east flank of the Front Range from Red Rocks to the
Garden of the Gods. Sedimentary layers, the remains
of the ancestral Rockies, have been stood on end by
the Front Range uplift and sculpted, carved and
smoothed, by the elements.

From Colorado Springs, take U.S. Hwy. 24 to
Woodland Park. As you enter Woodland Park, watch
for Pikes Peak Road; it's not well marked. In 1986 it
was just past a Diamond Shamrock service station on
the right side of the road. Turn right on Pikes Peak
Road and continue to Baldwin Street. Turn left on
Baldwin Steet and proceed past the high school.
Baldwin becomes Rampart Range Road. About 3 miles
from Hwy. 24, there is an intersection where there is
a sign that says Rampart Range Road 1 mile; turn to
the left and continue past the road to the Rampart
Reservoir and follow the signs toward Denver. You are
now on the north fork of Rampart Range Road.
In another 2 miles or so you will come to the intersection with Mt. Herman Road, the road to Monument. This is the place. Make a right, park along the
road, unload, and head toward Monument on Mt.
Herman Road, Forest Route 320.

The sign reads, "Danger — Narrow Winding
Mountain Road." It's really not that bad. This is an
all-weather gravel road. Start up a moderate grade
and after 0.2 miles begin an easy 1.0 mile descent. If
you build up a little speed you can stay in high gear
and climb up to the lookout at 1.4 miles. At 2.3 miles
you will come to the intersection with Forest Route
322.1; turn left onto 322.1 and continue through the

trees. The road is narrow and curvy; not bad though. The Air Force Academy is about 5 miles southeast of this point.

There is a moderate grade at 3.2 miles that builds up to a 20 percenter at 3.4 miles and then turns into a roller coaster series of ups and downs. Stay to the left on 322.1 at 3.9 miles. Forest Route 322.1 joins Forest Route 322 at around 4.0 miles. Route 322 is Balanced Rock Road. Turn left onto 322. You can only go left; to the right is the Palmer Lake Watershed and a closed road.

There is a grand view of Pikes Peak just after you make the turn onto 322. You'll see Pikes Peak for the next couple of miles.

There is some loose gravel on the road, but it is generally in pretty good shape. You'll have easy ups and downs all the way to Rampart Range Road at 6.2 miles. At Rampart Range Road make a left and proceed on a rolling, wide, gravel road back to the start.

*Monument on Monument Creek Road*

# A Appendix:
## Rank by Ride Rating

| # | Ride Description | Ride Rating | Skill Level | Page |
|---|---|---|---|---|
| 9 | Greenbelt Plateau | Easy | Beginning | 66 |
| 8 | Community Ditch Trail | Easy | Beginning | 62 |
| 26 | Waterton Canyon | Easy | Beginning | 138 |
| 10 | Winter Park Area — Vasquez Creek | Easy/ Moderate | Intermediate | 70 |
| 25 | Kuehster Road | Moderate | Beginning | 134 |
| 27 | Southern Front Range — Monument Creek Loop | Moderate | Beginning | 142 |
| 4 | Crown Point Road | Moderate | Beginning | 45 |
| 7 | Golden Gate Canyon State Park | Moderate | Beginning/ Intermediate | 58 |
| 22 | Kenosha Creek | Moderate | Intermediate | 121 |
| 12 | Hamlin Gulch | Moderate | Intermediate | 79 |
| 14 | West Chicago Creek Road | Moderate | Intermediate | 87 |
| 1 | Dowdy Lake Loop | Moderate | Intermediate | 32 |
| 2 | Manhattan Road to Swamp Creek | Moderate | Intermediate | 37 |
| 20 | Keystone Gulch to North Peak | Moderate/ Strenuous | Intermediate | 112 |

| # | Ride Description | Ride Rating | Skill Level | Page |
|---|---|---|---|---|
| **24** | Shawnee Reservoir | Moderate/ Strenuous | Intermediate | 130 |
| **17** | Old Squaw Pass Road | Moderate/ Strenuous | Intermediate | 100 |
| **6** | Eldora to Fourth of July Trailhead | Moderate/ Strenuous | Intermediate | 54 |
| **18** | Camp Rock — Mt. Evans State Wildlife Area | Moderate/ Strenuous | Intermediate | 104 |
| **15** | Devils Canyon Loop | Moderate/ Strenuous | Intermediate/ Advanced | 91 |
| **3** | Dadd Gulch Loop | Moderate/ Strenuous | Intermediate/ Advanced | 41 |
| **5** | Estes Park Area — House Rock | Strenuous | Intermediate | 50 |
| **21** | Montezuma Area — Webster Pass | Strenuous | Intermediate | 117 |
| **23** | Bill Tyler Gulch to Gibbs Gulch | Strenuous | Intermediate | 126 |
| **16** | Barbour Fork Loop | Strenuous | Intermediate/ Advanced | 95 |
| **11** | St. Marys Glacier to Yankee Hill | Strenuous | Advanced | 74 |
| **19** | Green Mountain | Strenuous | Advanced | 108 |
| **13** | Bard Creek Road | Strenuous | Advanced | 83 |

Priority was given to the "Ride Rating" over the "Skill Level" in ordering the rides listed on these two pages.

*Notes*

*Notes*

# About the Author

**William L. Stoehr** moved to Colorado six years ago from Wisconsin. He and his wife, Mary, own and run Trails Illustrated, and in addition to bicycling they like to ski and backpack. The Stoehr family lives in Evergreen.